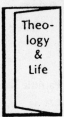

Theo-
logy
&
Life

THEOLOGY AND LIFE SERIES

Some New and Recent Titles

Other Titles in Preparation

A
Pilgrim God
for a
Pilgrim People

DENIS CARROLL

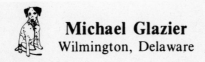
Michael Glazier
Wilmington, Delaware

ABOUT THE AUTHOR

Denis Carroll is a priest of the Archdiocese of Dublin. He lectures in Systematic Theology at Mater Dei Institute and at Trinity College, Dublin, His publications include *What is Liberation Theology?* and *Towards a Story of the Earth.*

BT
102
.C36
1989

First published in 1989 by Michael Glazier, Inc.,
1935 West Fourth Street, Wilmington, Delaware 19805,
by arrangement with Gill and Macmillan Ltd., Dublin.
© 1988 by Denis Carroll

Library of Congress Cataloging-in-Publication Data
Carroll, Denis.
    A pilgrim God for a pilgrim people / Denis Carroll.
        p. cm.
    ISBN 0-89453-749-0
    1. God.   2. Faith.   I. Title.
BT102.C36   1989   89-24596
231-dc19   CIP

Printed in Great Britain.

Cover Design by Lilian Brulc.

To my mother and father
who gave me life and love
and to those who have brought God to me
through beauty, love and truth

Contents

Introduction

WHAT follows will be little more than a stammer. However, no apology is offered. After all, Martin Buber reminded us many years ago that the root of the Hebrew term for God is itself a stutter-word. How can we speak coherently of what surpasses all our imagining. One can say—in Herbert McCabe's phrase—God matters. God matters to individuals. God matters to the societies they construct. God matters to the project of justice, peace and love symbolised by the 'kingdom of God'. And it was while writing this book that I came to know how important it is to be able to affirm that God matters to the dead as well as the living.

This study is part of the broader scheme of a pilgrim's theology. The milestones laid down by tradition are respected for the guidance they offer. Nonetheless, these milestones disclose that the pilgrim's road is never free of surprise. The road leads to new places, opens up new vistas. The book here introduced was written with the great symbols of Christian tradition in mind. It was written under the conviction that the most powerful renovation comes from the tradition itself. Hence, many of the questions taken up in contemporary theologies of liberation are dealt with here indirectly rather than directly. The theological critique of injustice arises through the withdrawal of legitimation from earthly powers in the death of Jesus at their hands. Likewise, the critique of racism, sexism and economic domination comes from the relationships of equality, mutual love and overbrimming joy glimpsed in a theology of Father, Son and Blessed Spirit. *This* Father, *this* Son, *this* Spirit cannot be made to underwrite imperialism whether economic, cultural, racial or sexual. Rather, God's passion for the life and flourishing of God's creation is the great denial of such imperialism.

Denis Carroll

1

No Easy Certitude

I

'God is not obvious even to Saints.'
Michael P. Gallagher[1]

THEOLOGY (Theos = God, Logos = Word) is always a risky business. Real speech about God is not purchased cheaply. It cannot be taken for granted. Whereas loose talk is to be avoided in every field, careless talk—or writing—about God can touch on blasphemy. The best coinage of speech about God is action or way of life. Hence arises the claim that right doing (*orthopraxis*) is more valuable than right speaking (*orthodoxy*). The medieval theologian, William of St Thierry, reminds us that in the approach to God our manner of life is more important than our manner of speech.[2]

How does one write about God? Are one's motives trivial? Are one's biases sufficiently examined? Many works commence with the protest of theological modesty and then contradict that avowal in page after confident page. Even this notice incurs the risk of immodesty—as if to say that whereas others may be unwittingly self-indulgent *here* everything will be controlled, discreet, austere.

There is a difference between speaking *to* God and speaking *about* God. Neither speech to God nor speech about God is light matter. Neither is to be undertaken flippantly. Both have to be attempted. To talk *to* God is always a permission and a grace. It yields refreshment and perhaps an experiential closeness to its object/subject. Talk *about* God runs the risk of arrogance, of escapism and of self-indulgence. The most we can plead in extenuation is that it is 'carried out in darkness or at best in twilight'.[3]

2

Perhaps the most tragic ignorance is to know—or to say—too much about God. Patrick Kavanagh's dry remark is elegantly understated: 'God [who] once all known becomes ridiculous'. There is a danger, then, that theology make God too available. Such a God is either trivial or illusory. God, when known, is hidden even in self disclosure. St Thomas Aquinas reminds us that even in the beatific vision God is greater than we can ever comprehend. An Asian theologian, Choan-Seng Song, has spoken of the shy God of Jesus Christ—the God who is present as much in secret unscheduled places as in luminous religious pretention. The much discussed crisis in the Churches has precipitated a theological reconsideration of the characteristics of faith. Today, faith in God: 'will be more searching than sure, more personal than institutional, more complex than simple, more a victory won in the teeth of defeat than an easy assumption of certitude'.[4] Bearing this in mind, one can nonetheless hold that speech about God *may* be a service to faith, hope and love. Ludwig Wittgenstein aphoristically remarks: 'of what cannot be said, thereof, one must be silent'.[5] However, silence is best as the silence of completion. On the way to that silence, one must say something.

II

'Believing means putting ones trust in someone who
to begin with still refuses to say who He is.'
Edward Schillebeeckx[6]

For a brief time, the 'death of God' was a dominant theme in European and North American theological writing. God was declared redundant. God, it was claimed, had become morally intolerable, intellectually superfluous and emotionally dispensable. 'Man come of age' could do without God. Either 'he' could act as if God did not exist (*etsi Deus non daretur*) or 'he' could go even further to avow with Stendhal that 'the only excuse for God is that he does not exist'. Yet, the 'death of God' soon ran out of date. It was quickly seen as theological suicide, a heroic but misguided self-destruction. The secular city was not consistently secular. It continued to seek out its

3

own gods. It is a particular irony, wryly noted by Andrew Greeley, that the sons and daughters of the secularised academicians undertook a new and often dangerous sacralisation by way of occultism, eastern religion and guru dependency.

On the other hand, the 'death of God' was a valuable reminder that 'God', as word, can become jaded, empty and devoid of meaning. There is an uncomfortable point to Nietzche's cry 'God is dead and we have killed him'. Henry de Lubac argues that advanced industrial society exercises an inexorable pressure towards the banishment of God. In the experience of absurdity, suffering and oppression there is much to justify the perception of 'the silence of God'. While refusing to admit the death of God, many convinced Christians will admit the death of the immediacy of God.[7] They will find it difficult to re-echo André Frossard's claim: 'God exists. I have met him.'[8] Can there be such a 'meeting' where everything is certain, obvious, stable and untroubled?

To distinguish the death of God from the death of the immediacy of God is more than a clever sleight of hand. There is a difference between declaring 'there is no God' and recognising that God eludes our beck and call. God is not in our pocket. God's action cannot be programmed. Pascal's remark is apt: 'a religion which does not affirm that God is hidden is not true'. Experience of history, of personal relationships, and of nature can disclose an emptiness, even an appalling cruelty. This negative experience may have driven many to say either regretfully or with relief: 'There is no God. God is dead.' With customary realism Karl Rahner has written: 'The real argument against Christianity is this experience of darkness. I have always found that behind the technical arguments levelled against Christianity there are always various experiences of life causing the spirit and the heart to be dark, tired and despairing.'[9]

On the other hand, the Judaeo-Christian tradition insists that God can be discerned in nature, in history, and in people. To make that insistence credible much detailed, patient work is required. One must respect the anguished cry that God could not exist since so much evil is rampant. One must try to offer an honest reply to the philosophic and social analyses which either assume the nullity of God or claim to have dis-

4

proved God's being. Above all, one must 'let God speak' in the varied ways to which the whole Judaeo-Christian tradition is meant to point.

This is work 'carried out in darkness or at best in twilight'.[10] Without anticipation of a face-to-face meeting it still looks for where God may be found. The Jewish experience of God was always *a tergo* (from behind). Yahweh went with the people but always ahead of them: 'you cannot see my face; you can see me only from behind' (Ex. 33:18-23). To know the divine name provided no power over God's inner mystery. Therefore, Israel's preferred name for God, Yahweh, retains an aura of reserve and of hiddenness, even in generous disclosure. The Judaeo-Christian faith proclaims 'God lives, God is not dead'. Yet, it also protests that God's living touch comes in the least predictable ways.

The admission that God is known in a certain absence shakes us from the lethargy of presumption and the inertia of routine. It pushes faith in God towards the openness of a pilgrim and away from the premature securities of immobility or settledness. The Old Testament depicts a pilgrim's nomadic faith rather than that of a sedentary grazier or tiller. This kind of faith keeps hearts ready and senses keen. It disallows rest in the consolations of pietism or of quietism. Thereby, it fosters the doing of justice and the action of transformative love. Edward Schillebeeckx claims: 'It is precisely this break with an 'immediate' relationship with God in faith which has opened the doors of our churches to political theology, to the origin of critical communities and to [the struggle for] a better world.'[11]

The hiddenness of God means that we do not control the knowledge of God. We must await ever-surprising glimpses of the glory of God. God is known in indirectness rather than in easy vision. Thus arises the principle of sacramentality, the knowledge of God through symbols and signs. All things can point to a God ever present yet elusive of our grasp. To use Peter Berger's phrase, we must look for 'signals of transcendence'. These call for a discernment which is neither pretentious nor facile. There is a price to this principle of sacramentality or mediation. What reveals God can also hide God. We know God only through the metaphors or models or masks which, we believe, offer a presence in absence. Even if metaphors or models or masks are God-given they remain all too human. Adrian Hastings rightly urges that 'the history of God is in part one of deciding which masks God can wear; which God can not'.[12] Such metaphors or models or masks are never too much ahead of the standards of their day.

III

'The God of theology is what we make Him.'

Bruce Vawter

All too often, humanity's worst—as well as best—instincts have been transferred to God. The cruelty, the oppression, even the repressed sadism in human history have sought their justification in God. The true prophets of all times have opposed this conscription of God to the service of vested interests. Despite their protest, Voltaire's caustic remark retains a certain point: God created man and man returned the compliment. The most telling objection today to the traditional affirmation of God is not that it presents a God 'up there' or 'out there'. It is rather that affirmations of God can be an alienating diversion or a subtle establishment of dominant interests. J. L. Segundo remarks: 'Our unjust society and our perverted idea of God are in close and terrible alliance'.[13]

The story is told of Sri Ramakrishna, a Hindu priest (1836-1886) who had a vision of God. In discussing Christ with his disciples, Sri Ramakrishna asked, 'tell me what the bible says about the features of Christ, what did he look like?' They answered, 'We have not seen this particularly mentioned anywhere in the bible; but Jesus was born among the Jews, so he must have been fair with large eyes and an acquiline nose.' The teacher remarked, 'But I saw his nose was a little flat—who knows why.' Not attaching much importance to those words at the time, the disciples, after his passing away, heard that there were three extant descriptions of Christ's features, and one of these actually described him as flat-nosed.[14]

It is noted that Christ did not appear to Ramakrishna as Semite or Anglo-Saxon or Arian. The 'flat nose' is associated with people of Asian or Mongolian extraction. An African bishop at the Roman Synod of 1985 remarked that God is

6

always presented as 'white' and never as 'black'. The point is that God must be allowed to be what God wants to be: the God of black or brown people as well as white; the God of the poor as well as of the rich; the God of women as well as of men; the God of all creation and not just of humankind.

The Irish Jesuit, George Tyrrell, once wrote that 'even our best God is an idol'.[15] Certainly, even our best God can *become* an idol. Our concepts and our words can become idolatrous if their susceptibility to manipulation is not kept in mind. Just as the corruption of the best is always the worst *(corruptio optimi pessima)* the abuse of God's name creates a hideous blasphemy and a deformation of humanity. St Thomas Aquinas makes a critical distinction between the way of signifying (*modus significandi*) and the thing signified (*res significata*). Nowhere is that distinction more necessary than in claims about God. It disqualifies the claim that any conception or statement about God can capture what God truly is.

IV

'If our Christian experience is really
authentic, then it must be a continuing
journey from atheism to faith.'

J. L. Segundo

Faith does not inhabit a risk-free zone. The affirmation of God is troubled by our own weakness and inability to rise to the demands it makes of us. Each day I must confront my own atheism as it cushions me against the demands of real Christianity. Theism is always beset by laziness, complacency and connivance at injustice. Understood as the dark side of our moral experience 'atheism is a necessary element of our faith'.[16] The affirmation of God is always stronger for the recognition that this underside exists. We have daily to regain the affirmation of God. Daily we have to conquer the temptation to deny or ignore the reality of God in our lives. In this sense atheism is part of the genesis of faith.

There is another challenge to the affirmation of God which, paradoxically, grows out of the affirmation itself. Here the challenge is raised in the very name of faith. There are

7

experiences where faith makes it impossible to believe! These experiences evoke justified outrage in the face of innocent suffering. There is the random strike of disease. There are the vast cruelties of history. Some are known to us. Others remain submerged, for the story of the suffering is frequently edited out of recorded history by the victors. There are the multiple tragedies of our own day. Gregory Baum asks: 'If there is room in divine providence for the holocaust can we believe in such a God?'[17] This is not atheism in the sense mentioned in the preceeding paragraph. Richard Rubenstein's declaration of atheism must be placed against such a backdrop. In *After Auschwitz* his protest of atheism is a remonstrance with God in God's own name and by God's own people. In *Answer to Job*, Carl Gustav Jung explores the protest which the reflective mind will raise against God on account of God's own principles. According to Jung, Job's complaint seems morally preferable to God's arbitary display of might. Why does the innocent man suffer? Why is the principle of evil given free rein? Many will concur with Jung's argument: 'a more differentiated consciousness must . . . find it difficult to love God as a kind father, a God whom on account of his unpredictable fits of rage, his unreliability, injustice and cruelty, it has every reason to fear'.[18]

Today, faith in God cannot be untroubled. Faith must cry out against the seeming wantonness in nature. It must contest the profligacy in human interaction so costly in thwarted lives and endless suffering. Against an untroubled religion one must object: 'For the very reason these men do not weep, there is something false in their rejoicing.'[19] A troubled theism, disturbing though it may be, is a healthy growth. It is not to be suppressed but rather assimilated and integrated into the movement of a more critical faith. In its very bleakness, a troubled theism can lead to an authentic dismantling of the idols fashioned by oneself and by one's tradition.

V

The Protest of Atheism

Atheism takes many forms. It arises from diverse motivation. The Second Vatican Council admitted that: 'taken as a whole, atheism is not a spontaneous development, but stems from a variety of causes, including a critical reaction against religious beliefs, and in some cases against the Christian religion in particular'.[20] Atheism, therefore, is not a seamless robe. Certainly, it is the denial of the existence of God. Yet it can also be the denial of the worthwhileness of the God represented by believers as individuals and the Church as a collectivity. The outline of modern atheism discloses several routes by which people come—or rather are driven—to that denial. The atheism of a Karl Marx is not the same as that of the liberal Enlightenment. Neither of these is the same as the anguished rejection which an individual may utter in the wake of 'the wintry experience of God' (Donal Dorr). Again, people have been branded as atheists when nothing could be further from their meaning and their intention. In this loose way, Paul Tillich, A. N. Whitehead, J. A. T. Robinson and even Pierre Teilhard de Chardin have been accused of atheism.

The onset of secularisation—in itself a positive development—has progressively called in question the value of appealing to God as a principle of explanation. Occam's Razor—'it is void to do with more what can be done with fewer'—disqualifies the appeal to a supernatural or a divine explanation where another explanation can be given. The 'God of the Gaps' does justice neither to God nor to the development of human responsibility. Thus has occurred a retreat from the claim that God intervenes in natural processes as one force amongst others. God is not the explanatory reason for earthquakes, thunderstorms, bad or good weather. God does not appear to threaten or to cajole or to praise. God is not the cause of maladies (by way of punishment) or of cures (by way of reward). The secularised consciousness will rightly expect natural causes to 'explain' natural effects. God will not do as a hypothesis of explanation. One can say without irreverence that science—and several other human endeavours—can get along splendidly without God. This kind of methodological atheism is distinct from atheism proper.

Yet, it is a short step from the methodological—and altogether correct—omission of God from scientific theory to an ideological affirmation of the superfluousness of God. In a science-dominated culture it is all too easy to declare God redundant. To do so is always fallacious. Just as the existence of God cannot be established as a scientific conclusion, neither can it be disproved by scientific argument. When such a disproof is raised in the name of science it is exorbitant and ideological. It expresses the view of the scientist himself/herself rather than the valid result of scientific reasoning.

An argument adduced for such denial is the sufficiency of the universe as its own explanation. It is argued that no further explanation is needed than the fact of the universe. To cite Bertrand Russell: 'the universe is just there and that's all'. Against this, one can argue that scientific atheism injects a form of explanatory principle to the universe. It, too, moves into the question of sense or meaning. Just as surely as theist metaphysics, it entertains the question, 'Why is there being rather than nothing?' In effect, it postulates an inherent rationality to the universe over and above the rationality of its parts. An example is the mixture of chance and necessity postulated by the Nobel prize-winner Jacques Monod. Others speak of evolutionary finality, of historical determinism and of the potentiality of matter. There is an inconsistency here. A creative power with Godlike attributes is surreptitiously introduced. John Macquarrie remarks: 'The more atheism imports into matter in the way of form, creativity, direction and so on, the nearer it moves to pantheism and an immanent quasi God'.[21]

Another strand of atheism—perhaps, more congenial to modern Christian sentiment—originates in protest. Its classic statement is the metaphysical rebellion of Albert Camus. Arising from anger at a creation ridden by pain, injustice and absurdity, it refuses to endorse any promise of other-worldly compensation or vindication. For this kind of protest, the supreme blasphemy is not the denial of God but the consolation offered, for instance, in Schiller's *Ode to Joy:*

> Be patient, O millions!
> Be patient for the better world!
> There above the starry sky
> A great God will give a reward.[22]

Thus Doestoevsky's Ivan Karamazov rejects creation in the

name of the suffering child: 'If the sufferings of children go to make up the sum of sufferings which is necessary for the purchase of truth, then I say beforehand that the entire truth is not worth such a price.'[23] Many studies advert to the several images of God depicted in the protest atheism of literature and theatre: God is the deceiver, sadist, despot. Or again, God is erring, helpless, bored, asleep. These are provocative images of protest to ignore which would be folly.[24]

It is always folly to minimise the protest against religion made in the name of humaneness. There is an 'emergent humanism of liberty' which questions the compatibility of affirming God with the cherishing of humankind. Can we live maturely and responsibly in the presence of this all-seeing subject? Is God not the negation of human subjectivity and freedom? Does 'he' not 'transform everything into a mere object, a thing among things, a cog in the machine?'[25] In line with this critique, a denial of God is uttered in the name of psychological wholeness, of political responsibility, even of scientific freedom.

One final objection remains to be considered: the protest against God in the name of the injustices done in God's name. What is being rejected here? Is it not the God with the aquiline nose? The God of the conquistadores or whoever the modern conquistador may be? J. L. Segundo points out that 'an indictment of the social system necessarily leads one to criticise a notion of God which is the projection of a false image created by an ideology of domination'.[26] When Christians say 'I believe', it is possible that they are making an act of faith in capitalism, injustice or egoism.

Conversely, when others say 'I don't believe', they may be denying the validity of capitalism or injustice or egoism. They may be affirming that another way is conceivable where a definitive reversal of greed, inhumaneness, cruelty and selfishness takes place. Thus, there is a rejection of God in the name of something higher than the alienating masks which God is made to bear. Atheism can then be: 'a demanding and noble cause fired with enthuasism and idealism, dreaming of justice and progress and striving for a social order [conceived of] as the ultimate perfection'.[27]

Common to all these rejections is a stress on God's

11

intolerableness rather than God's metaphysical impossibility. For humankind to be, God must die. Is this a pathological version of the Oedipus complex or a valid protest in the name of humanity? It can be argued that the protest of atheism has not succeeded in fashioning an alternative where humankind is cherished, where rights are observed and dignity respected. Indeed, the most appalling atrocities of our time—the holocaust and the concentration camps—occurred under regimes professing atheism. Hence, atheism either as a programme or as a protest itself has questions to answer. Does the denial of God negate the human creativity it was intended to serve? Does it unleash demonic forces in the human spirit? T. S. Eliot has written of the consequences of the widespread rejection of God —

> ...what have we to do
> but stand with empty hands and palms turned upwards
> in an age which advances progressively backwards[28]

Yet granted all this, those who affirm the God of theism would do well to consider what in their own affirmation evokes the protest. At what point does the God of theism mask the compassionate God of Jesus Christ?

VI

The New Right
'The sparring partner (of faith in God) will no longer be an atheism that has become exhausted after a century spent in an all too disappointing exercise of power—but several varieties of neo-paganism that challenge both the nationalist inheritance of the Enlightenment and the Judaeo-Christian faith .'

André Dumas[29]

Doubtless, 'new right' is an overstretched term. For one thing, it gets applied to quite diverse currents of thought. In the context of this study, it designates a post-modern, affluent, northern—hemispheric phenomenon. Its spokespersons are found in business, in politics, in journalism and in the entertainment industry. In France, the writings of Louis Pauwels

12

(Le Droit de Parler) and Alain de Benoist *(Vu de Droite)* are good examples of the philosophy of the new right. This philosophy is articulated in various ways in the United States, Germany, Spain and Great Britain. As distinct from the older philosophies of the right, it does not seek an accommodation with Christianity. Without metaphysical commitment, it nonetheless affirms a multitude of deities, rituals and myths.

The 'new right' rejects the God of Christianity because of God's perceived identification with the poor, the weak and the powerless. Already framed by Nietzsche, the charge is raised once again that Christianity is the crutch of the miserable and the 'resentful'. The 'new right' is deeply inimical to compassion. It detests any kind of messianism or utopian vision of change. The aspiration to shape history in the direction of justice and fair play is rejected out of hand. Instead, protagonists of the 'new right' argue that 'now' is all there is. They emphasise the individualistic, cynical and pragmatic injunction: *carpe diem* (make the most of today). A commentator on this movement, André Dumas, warns: 'When neopaganism is really unleashed, we know that its innocence is in fact cruelty, its abolition of sin is association with the abyss, and its contempt for forgiveness is man's destruction.'[30]

This current of thought is mentioned here because of its affinity with the dominant values of advanced capitalist society. It pitches its allure to a more affluent and diversion-seeking youth. It represents the cult not of excellence but of success, of efficiency, of power, of achievement in politics, industry, sport and, even, sex. The new right reserves its most lively contempt for that strand within Christianity which presses for social transformation in the direction of justice. Lacking the nobility of the atheism of protest, the self-centred religion of the 'new right' may indeed be said to be the sharpest antithesis to a prophetic confession of the living God.

VII

Critique from within

In a widely noticed study, published in 1935, E. Petersen argued that belief in God all too frequently was used to

13

underpin monarchies and empires.[31] Petersen instanced the virtual equivalence made by Constantine's court theologian, Eusebius of Caesarea, of the *lex constantina* to the law of God. The divine right of kings—surely a pernicious doctrine—explicitly derives from an arrogation of divine sanction. In a recent essay, David Nichols suggested that a dominant model in Christianity has been of God as all powerful, albeit benevolent, administrator. Clearly, the acceptance of this model is liable to subserve the stability of both civil and ecclesiastical establishments.[32] The misuse of the name of God to buttress vested interests has dogged Christianity in east and west like a dark shadow. To lay hands on 'God power' seems an inevitable temptation in every society where religion attains corporate expression. And so it is claimed that the prevalence of models of God as monarch, ruler, omnipotent creator has not been an unmixed blessing. These models have been used to ensure compliance with unjust social structures. Likewise, they have smothered the articulation of alternative experiences of God by marginalised groups whether these be poor, or non-white, or female. Thus, the 'subversive memory'* set into the scriptures was tamed. It was forgotten more than once that the God of the Old Testament was partial to the oppressed in opposition to the dominant and the powerful. Again, it was forgotten that Jesus of Nazareth was executed as an outcast, a criminal and a disturber.

It should be noted that this criticism arises from within faith in God. The theology of liberation practised in South America and Asia highlights the ideological abuse of the name of God. A hidden agenda can prevail even in the most solemn pronouncements both of theologians and of church leaders. José Comblin points out that 'theologians must eat before doing theology. Thus they see the world through the eyes of those who guarantee them their daily bread.'[33] Leonardo Boff reminds us that 'the church has often become the legitimating religious ideology for the imperial social order'.[34] Where this happens, the true God can be replaced by a God of the generals, the juntas and the landowners.

*This phrase, now associated with the work of J. B. Metz, reminds us that the Old Testament was haunted by a memory of servitude overcome through God's liberative concern for oppressed people. It is a memory subversive of subsequent oppression whether that oppression comes from within the people of Israel or from outside.

Theologians sensitive to holistic, ecological thinking, also mount a critique of images and models of God, in some respects even more radical than that of Liberation theology. Process theology charts the insufficiency of the images of God as overseer of the moral order, the manipulator of puppet-like creatures, the monarch who rules in distant grandeur. Process theologians see these 'pictures' as typical of the traditional presentation of God. They move away from such 'pictures' and emphasise the compassionate God intrinsic to cosmic processes while not identical with them. A. N. Whitehead, John Cobbe and Norman Pittenger attempt to rethink the nature of a God sympathetic with an evolving creation and present to it at all stages of its development.[35] In doing so they push mainstream theology to reconsider its ways of imaging God.

Somewhat similarly—although much more concretely—feminist theologians contest the patriarchal images and models of God in the traditional expression of Judaeo-Christianity. These theologians enter their protest as a service to the liberation of people from excessively patriarchal categories. They emphasise the distortions brought about within theology through the predominance of patriarchal models. As did theologians of liberation so feminist theologians uncover the operation of vested interests in this distortion. They stress that the structures of patriarchy have a large stake in the perpetuation of such God-models. Mary Daly's aphorism has become notorious: 'Where God is male, there male is God.' White, ruling class, imperialist, male interests become God's interests.

VIII

'God does not die on the day when we cease to
believe in a personal deity, but *we* die on
the day when our lives cease to be illuminated
by the steady radiance... of a wonder, the
source of which is beyond all reason.'
Dag Hammarskjold

A human being can never be totally limited by his or her environment. *Anima capax omnium* runs the old adage—the human spirit thrusts beyond every immediate attainment or achievement. In its unremitting desire for the good and the true the spirit evidences its own uniqueness. This is certainly a desire for what Christians term eternal life. It is a desire for communion with a truth surpassing all partial truths, a good supportive of all partial goods, a love originative of all loves. Christian theology of all traditions calls this Truth, Love and Good, God. Tertullian, that magnificently turbulent father of the Church, claimed that the human spirit is naturally Christian —*anima naturaliter christiana*. Less specifically, one may claim that the spirit is naturally religious—*anima naturaliter religiosa*. Many factors threaten to smother that natural 'endowment' yet the dynamic relationship of created spirit to Creator perdures.

In his lively study *The Persistence of Religion*, Andrew Greeley claims that our basic religious needs have not changed notably since the late Ice Age.[36] Greeley contests the view that 'man come of age' can dispense with the ultimate. In his view, 'secularised man' is to be found mainly in *academia* and, even then, amongst *academia's* more senior inhabitants. The young all too frequently are lured to cultic practices, esoteric religions, astrology and tarot cards. Greeley argues that the sacred—the real or imagined transcendent dimension— is not easily cut away. In Europe and North America, the prevalent interest in witchcraft, the occult and para-psychology may indicate boredom, self-indulgence and decadence. Nonetheless, a wise theological and pastoral reflection will not ignore its challenge.

This reading in the sociology of religion is confirmed in the writings of C. G. Jung. From the perspective of clinical psychology and psychotherapy Jung came to believe that the suppression of religious symbolisms lies at the root of much psychological disease. In his study, *The Psychology of the Unconscious*, Jung speaks of the recurrent presentation by patients of what comparative religion has shown to be universal symbols for the divinity. Whereas Freud related every symptom to repressed sexuality, Jung postulated an undifferentiated thrust or energy in search of rebirth or healing. He came to speak of 'an archetype of wholeness' to which all other archetypes are related. The archetype of wholeness occupies so central a position in the subconscious mind that it can be approximated to the God-image. Jung would have us realise that whether we be believers or non-believers, these residual memories operate in our psyche. He reminds us that 'When God is not recognised selfish desires develop and out of this selfishness comes illness'. And again: 'wherever the spirit of God is excluded from human consideration, an unconscious substitute takes its place'—a state, a leader, a party, a neighbour, ourselves.[37] In this direction lies not liberation or wholeness, but a veritable hell on earth.

Neither Greeley's sociological indications nor Jung's psychological considerations are probative of the God of faith. As scientist, Jung disclaims any especial competence in either the proof or the disproof of God. A prevalent interest in cults, astrology, the I Ching or the Enneagram may simply argue to dilettantism, diversion and boredom. Such an interest does not justify a revival of uncritical religious practices or the restoration of old-time religion. Again, the psychological considerations from Jungian psychology, apparently corroborative of the affirmation of God, can be matched by Sigmund Freud's strictures on the illusory nature of religion. For Freud 'illusion' is a belief—whether true or false—where wish fulfilment is a prominent factor in its motivation. Freud regarded religion as a wish fulfilment based on pathological foundations. The withering of religion would be something to be desired, a sign of improvement and progress.

Tertullian's aphorism, mentioned earlier, finds a repeated echo in theology. It finds particular reference in the medieval stress upon the natural desire for God. This 'natural desire' is not to be equated with the Jungean libido although the comparison has been made. Rather, it argues that the human spirit is a high point of God's creation, made to find union with God as deepest fulfilment. Augustine's words summate it well: 'Thou hast made us for thyself O God and our hearts are not content until they rest in thee.' In recent years, Henri de Lubac and Karl Rahner have developed this theme to construct a theological view of humanity inescapably oriented towards the mystery of God. Rahner claims: 'The knowledge of God is inevitably present in the depths of existence in the most ordinary human life.'[38] Since man/woman are in search of God,

17

whether they recognise that quest or not, the acknowledgment of God remains indispensable for humankind. Conversely, where the acknowledgment of God dies out upon the earth an essential characteristic of our humanity will have disappeared: 'The absolute death of the word God (however it is cast)...would be the signal...that man had died.'[39]

This view contests both militant atheism and atheism by default. Wherever atheism is raised to a system, its ultimate success entrains the mutilation of the person. Just as state religion leads to the death of God, state atheism leads to the death of man. Were systematic atheism ever to succeed, essential needs of the person would be suppressed. The consciousness of an inalienable dignity as a child of God, the hope of eternal life, the awareness of a transcendence of time and space given with spirituality, these irreplaceable elements of our human inheritance are excised only by force. In the same way, atheism by default would bespeak a humanity which had lost itself. It would spell capitulation to the shoddy values of consumerism, a willingness to settle for a 'mess of pottage' unworthy of humankind and ultimately destructive of it. This destruction of humanness is at the heart of Hammarskjold's warning with which this section commenced.

IX

The reflections so far offered move in several directions. They recommend a modesty in theological claims. Yet they also highlight the need to speak theologically. They touch on a religious dimension set into our very humanity. On the other hand, they advert to a troubled theism, to that moment in the act of faith where the possibility of atheism is startlingly real. Above all, they advert to the need for a continual renewal of our thinking and speaking about God. Otherwise, we lose the alertness to the new which living faith is meant to carry. Here indeed is the value of St Thomas's insistence that the highest knowledge of God is reached when we can sincerely profess that God is above all our knowing. With that profession is attained the confluence of thought, prayer and adoration.

The theological series, of which this study is but one link, is aptly entitled 'Theology of a Pilgrim People'. It requires effort to avow that one is a pilgrim: that one's clan, tribe, nation or race is on the move, does not have a monopoly of wisdom or virtue. In terms of theological discourse it requires even greater effort to allow that God is disclosed as a pilgrim God. It is much easier to rest content with pieties already attained, to cleave to securities which ward off disturbance and doubt. Yet, the painful realisation of pilgrimage is forced on us from several quarters. The biblical record is no longer seen as a monolithic, static once-for-all view of God. On the contrary, many 'theologies' are found there which correct each other and remind us that the mystery of God is never fully penetrated. Again, from philosophy, from depth psychology and from the critical social sciences comes a costly purification. These sources highlight the alienation latent in our use of God. At first blush one is edged towards atheism.

We do well to advert to the possibility that it is not intellectual difficulties but rather shoddy witness to God which drives many people from the Churches. And so we have to look again at our *theo-logy*. In adverting to the changing 'masks' of God we must beware of casting God as a type of chameleon which changes its appearance in accordance with its environment or, to change the metaphor, 'a fox of heaven forever outpacing the pursuit of human hounds'. God must not always be the God of the newest gap. For then 'it would be a case of God yesterday and tomorrow but never God today'.[40]

2

By My Deeds Shall You Know Me

I

THE Old Testament presents the reader with a theological witness which, both in form and content, is a late development. The Book of Genesis represents the fusion of several traditions effected in late exilic or post-exilic times (fifth century B.C.). In common with Deutero-Isaiah and Ezechiel, Genesis has a very precise aim. Its purpose is to give a disheartened people adequate motive to hold on to their faith in God. Genesis rallies this depressed and dispirited group to a renewal of hope in the promise made of old to their ancestors. To this end, the history of Israel's election is retold: the call of Abraham, the promise made to him and its first fruits. As its name suggests, Genesis tells the story of Israel's coming to be. In prosecution of this task the narrative links the history of the Jewish people to the very creation of the world itself. This move is not unique in the history of religions. In their tribal or ethnic mythology, many ancient peoples attempt to link the tribe or people with absolute beginnings. Nevertheless, the connection of Israel's history with the coming-to-be of the world, made in the opening chapters of Genesis, is entirely coherent with the emergent awareness that the God of Israel was indeed the God of all people and that, through Israel, God would be saviour of all.

It is a commonplace now to admit the multiplicity of literary forms employed in the Bible. An extensive list includes saga, legend, myth, poetry, historical narrative, prophetic discourse, and apocalyptic vision. We have, perhaps, reached the stage where the word 'myth' no longer evokes the suspicion of untruth or debasement. Van A. Harvey has valuably reminded us that 'myth does not mean a false story but a highly selective story that is used to structure and convey the basic self-understanding of a person and a community'.[1] In the book of Genesis, material dealing with the origin of the cosmos is skilfully put to use. An account of how the universe came to be is offered in the relatively polished categories of mythic discourse. We do little justice to the subtlety of Genesis if we try to fit its opening chapters within the bounds of 'straight' narrative history. It is not to be taken as history but rather as symbol-laden narrative. It touches on issues central to the perennial human quest: the relation of the here-and-now to the utterly transcendent, the question of origins, of suffering, of sin and evil.

Yet, the difference between Genesis and the myths of the surrounding culture should not be minimised. The Genesis creation-narratives are solidly embedded in the theological history of Israel. The narrative is guided by the theology of the school of Ezechiel and Deutero-Isaiah to which the authors of Genesis would seem to belong. Hence, all trace of polytheism is absent. The lurid multiplicity of gods found in the *Epic of Gilgamesh* and the *Enuma Elish* is avoided. Yahweh-Elohim is the giver of life to all things. No rival principle, no competing god is prior to God's creative action. Creation is thoroughly good and entrusted in generous measure to human stewardship. Evil is acknowledged and the fact of moral shortfall is minutely detailed. In the several contexts where a 'fall' is mentioned, human wrong-doing or human weakness is seen to play a large part. There is no admixture of evil in Yahweh-Elohim.

There is another major difference between the opening eleven chapters of Genesis and the cosmogonic myths of comparable societies. It is the historic thrust found even in the creation accounts of Genesis. Cosmogony is not presented here for its own sake. G. Von Rad has argued that there is an annexation of creation 'history' to subserve an understanding of Israel's history: 'presumptuous as it may seem, creation is part of the aetiology of Israel'.[2] While Genesis 1-11 should not be taken any more literally than the normal dynamic of mythic discourse, nevertheless the context of these chapters roots them in that historical relationship with God for the under-

21

standing of which we are so much indebted to the Old Testament.

There is a delicate balance to the Genesis presentation of God. The peculiar combination of mythic discourse with the discourse arising from centuries-old oral traditions about God's choice of Israel, yields what E. Voegelin calls 'world history'. This kind of discourse exceeds both myth and history. As distinct from the timeless circularity of myth, it contains a reference to the historical dimension of existence. On the other hand, it has the symbolic multivalence lacking in historical narrative. Genesis respects both the divine transcendence and the divine immanence. It emphasises that Yahweh-Elohim is the God of all places and people as well as the God of Israel. It reflects the hope of a pilgrim people who, even in failure and infidelity, followed the promise made by Yahweh-Elohim. The editors of the Genesis narrative recognise that the God of the promise to Abraham is also the one who created 'in the beginning'. The God of the fathers is the Lord of all.

This turn to the historical should not obscure the evidence for an experience of God in nature which underlies the Genesis creation accounts. Israel experienced the creative presence of God in 'darkness and light, rain and snow, camel and hippopotamus, moon and stars, in the beauty of flowers, plants and animals, in the birth of a child'.[3] This theme is taken up in Psalm 8:

> When I see the heavens, the work of your hands,
> the moon and the stars which you arranged ...
> How great is your name, O Lord our God through all the
> earth!

And Psalm 19 evinces an impressive creation spirituality:

> The heavens proclaim the glory of God
> and the firmament shows forth the work of his hands.
> Day unto day takes up the story
> and night unto night makes known the message.

Historical apprehension does not choke out appreciation of God's presence in nature. The experience of God's dealings with Israel throughout the history of the covenant is linked to

22

the experience of God's lordship of the universe. It is likely that the trauma of exile, humiliation and defeat enabled the linkage to be made. Hence, Deutero-Isaiah and Ezechiel root the covenant with Israel in God's creativity. In these books there is a breakthrough from a faith always in danger of degenerating into tribal arrogance towards a faith with a global vision of God as Lord of all.

Through all its pages, the Old Testament speaks of God. It records faith in the living God who creates, who enters covenant relationship, who keeps faith from generation to generation. Cumulatively, the Old Testament is a story of human strength and weakness, pain and puzzlement, faith and infidelity. The story centres on hope for a way of life in the presence of God. This hope is gradually expanded to touch on life after death. According to John Shea, the Bible's story is 'a tale of God's intentions, His unswerving fidelity to the purposes of His creation'.[4]

In many different ways the Old Testament answers the questions not only of its own time but even those of our own day. From within our search for a God of compassion, of justice and of promise, we discern new depths in this biblical tale of God's creative compassion, of promise and of justice. Our pilgrimage can link to the biblical pilgrimage. One speaks of discovering *new* depths in the biblical tale. Yet, our address to these texts will have been motivated by our situation within the Judaeo-Christian tradition. The hunger for justice and exploitation-free living which the Old Testament evinces speaks to our present-day hunger for hope and justice. The biblical answer to this hunger of ours is that of a God who also is hungry for wholeness and justice. The creation narratives assure us of God's care for every scrap of reality and of God's approval of it as 'very good'. These narratives present the special character of man/woman as image of God. The creation given into our care for responsible stewardship is to be cherished and developed rather than despoiled and destroyed. God is the God of wholeness, of integrity, of a good creation.

The book of Exodus, especially, speaks to us not because of the accessibility of its signs and wonders to historical analysis but because of the concerns and intentions of the God it presents: 'Justice is the very life of God in man, God's redemptive involvement in our pain.'[5] This record of faith is indeed selective. It bears its own share of national or tribal ideology. We need not dwell over long on 'what precisely happened', although the critical exigence will not allow this question to be suppressed. Rather, from the standpoint of today, we seek out the clues to God's ways in the privileged record of another time and place.

II

The many names of God

'God is that common name which becomes a personal
name only when it is addressed to that unique
being who bears no name—then it becomes
prayer, invocation and request.'

Gerhard Von Rad[6]

Comparative religion discloses a wide diversity in name and concept for the divinity. Egyptian, Assyrian-Babylonian, Phoenician, Greek, Indian, Chinese and Aztec divinities could provide the material for a lexicon of divine names. There are the religions of ancient Gaul, of Rome, of Germanic lands. There are the many divinities of Celtic religion. Can a general classification make these concepts and names point to one ultimate reality? Do they all contain their grain of truth or are they evidence of humankind's tragic search for an ever elusive really real. The opposition between the God of faith and the myriad gods of religion is no longer seen as satisfactory. This kind of separation, favoured by Karl Barth, takes insufficient account of the slow painful discovery of the God of faith. Arrogantly it dismisses the religious quest and faith-achievement of people who had never the opportunity to acknowledge the God of Jesus Christ.

The names we give to the God of Judaeo-Christianity have a multiple linguistic derivation. 'God' has a Germanic root and is of pre-Christian origin. Etymologically, it refers to 'a being who is invoked', 'a being to whom sacrifice is offered'. The latin languages carry the names Dieu, Dio, Dios, all of which come from Deus. This latter word is said to have a Sanskrit root (Di) with the meaning 'to gleam'. The Greek Theos is

24

variously traced to *thein* (to provide), *aithein* (to burn or consume), and *theasthai* (to see all things).[7]

Elohim, the generic Semitic name for the divine, is expressive of God's greatness. The singular form (El) is normally used with a qualifier: El Shaddai (God the most high), El Kadosh (God the holy one), El 'Olam (the God of old time), El Elyon (God of the high places). Many exegetes argue that the great patriarchs—Abraham, Isaac and Jacob—knew El Shaddai but not the sacred tetragrammaton, Yahweh. The argument rests on the text at Exodus 6:3: 'God spoke to Moses and said: I am the Lord. I appeared to Abraham, to Isaac, and to Jacob as Almighty God, but I did not make myself known to them by my holy name.' It may be that these patriarchs were henotheists rather than monotheists. They worshipped, that is to say, El or Elohim as the God of their clan or tribe without an explicit affirmation that this was the *only* God.

The great biblical name is without doubt JHWH. It is the 'ineffable tetragramaton', the name of four consonants. In Hebrew usage, the missing vowels have to be supplied by the reader. Thus the mystery of the name is heightened. We do not know exactly how it was pronounced when it first came alive. Its linguistic ground is Yah, Yahu, Yo, Yeho. The French exegete Henri Cazelles, has pointed out that the semitic world did have a personal name for the divinity even before Israel became a nation: Yahu, Yau or Ya. Martin Buber has consistently argued that JHWH or one of its cognates was known even before Moses. Moses's introduction of the name JHWH to the Hebrew captives would have linked to a previous faith. 'The God of the Fathers' of Exodus 3 would then refer not simply to Elohim but to JHWH. In his work, *The Prophetic Faith,* Buber holds that although prior to Moses people used the Name they knew neither the character of God nor the full significance of that Name. It was the Exodus which gave new content to 'that tabu-word, that God cry, that stammering'—JHWH.[8]

The name JHWH is recorded in monumental evidence from the ninth century B.C. The stele of Mesha (found at Tell ed-Duweir, Palestine, 1933) dates from that time. It corroborates that the divine name JHWH was already current when, some time in the eighth century B.C., the account of the Exodus was committed to writing. The letters of Lakish (exchanged between a local military governor and his subordinates, after 597 and before 587) provided another later but extra-biblical evidence of the use of the name JHWH.

The 'post-exilic silence' has frequently been remarked upon by biblical scholarship. After the Babylonian exile a subtle change occurred whereby Leviticus 24:16 became a veto on pronunciation of the divine name rather than on blasphemy of that name.[9] Thus arises the circumlocution Adonai (in Greek translation, Kyrios, and in Latin, Dominus; in English, Lord). Instead of risking the pronunciation of the ineffable JHWH, Adonai was written and spoken. The alternative usage, Jehovah, in all probability derives from a masoretic text of the sixth century AD while some claim that Jehovah is no earlier than the sixteenth century AD.

The sacred name JHWH. There is an immense literature on the meaning of the divine name given in the episode of the burning bush. The narrative itself is highly dramatic. It is part of the greater Exodus story and not to be wrenched from that context. Moses, now a fugitive, is out in the desert. Suddenly he sees a bush which burns but is not consumed. Moses leaves his path and draws near. Then follows a vocation presented in the biblical model of call and response. God announces God's concern for the suffering of the Hebrews and sends Moses on a liberative mission to them. The only authentication given to the mission is God's own name. When Moses further asks what is this name, the great disclosure is given: I am who I am.

There are many ways of casting the name: I am who am: I am who I am; I am who I will be. Each version is a legitimate translation of the original text. The choice of one or other will say much about the theology of the chooser. Rather than tediously follow these variations it is proposed here to examine four samples of the major options of interpretation. They exemplify that even a critically established biblical text leaves much to the interpreter. The 'circle' of text and question to the text is nowhere more clearly instanced than here. Approaching the foundational text at Exodus 3 with our understanding of God fashioned by the intervening tradition of over three thousand years, we are enabled to enter the horizon opened up by it for faith in God through the ages. And so, a brief word will be offered on (*a*) a metaphysical, (*b*) a personal, (*c*) a mystical and (*d*) a historical understanding of Exodus 3:14.

Many versions translate the divine name as I am who Am. A primary warrant for this is the Greek (Septuagint) translation: Ego Eimi, and the Latin (Vulgate): Ego Sum Qui Sum. The medieval theologians discerned here an overtone of the infinite creativity of God. St Thomas Aquinas understands the divine name to express God's subsistent being, communicative of self, creative of everything that lives, moves and has being. For those who prefer this translation there is the added corroboration that JHWH relates to the Hebrew verb *to be, Hayah*. Further, the Hebrew construction at Exodus 3:16 can be translated as 'I am the one who causes to be whatever comes into existence.' Etienne Gilson, therefore, discerns a metaphysics of aseity (subsistent, independent being) in this text of Exodus. The modern reader of Exodus 3 can, accordingly, appeal to the text as support for his/her faith in God the giver of existence, the support or ground of personal being.

There is, however, a second option. For want of a better description it is here termed a 'personalist' understanding of the text. This reading of Exodus 3 sees JHWH as concerned for the well being of specific persons. Martin Buber speaks of the I-thou metaphysics of the Bible. JHWH is a personal God who can be with and for people. The God of the fathers is the God of people (*numen personale*) rather than a God of a shrine or sacred place (*numen locale*). JHWH is the God of Abraham, Isaac and Jacob, not the God of a spring or stone or mysterious holy place. God is not tied to any location. God is free to go with, to be present to the people. And so, when people today emphasise that God is personal through and through rather than neutrally impersonal, they can appeal to the perspective opened up by Exodus 3:14—I am who am for you and for my people.

There is a third approach to the interpretation of Exodus 3:14. This understanding discerns a refusal by God to yield up the divine name. For Hebrew thinking, power over the name was power over the person. And so, for Judaism the name of God must remain the preserve of God. God must remain hidden and transcendent. God's name cannot be the possession of any creature. With this in mind, Karl Barth claims that 'according to the most probable interpretation...[Exodus 3:14]...consists in a refusal of the name.'[10] Other exegetes argue that Exodus 3:14 is an evasive response to Moses' impetuous enquiry. The living God of Exodus remains above every attempt—even the most praise-worthy—to comprehend the nature of God. Exodus 3:14, then, evidences a refusal to disclose God's secret to any enquirer. The name of God remains above human utterance. *Nomen Dei est super omne nomen.* For such a tradition of understanding, Exodus 3:14 is best translated: I am (and remain) who I am (above every attempt to sound out the mystery).

The fourth reading of Exodus 3:14 may be said to carry the full resonance of the text. The Hebrew construction is indeterminate in regard to time or duration. Past, present and future action are simultaneously evinced by the one verb. Noting this, many exegetes translate *eyeh asher eyeh* in terms of continuing action. God was, is, and will be with God's people. the divine presence in the past to Abraham, Isaac and Jacob, the divine presence now to Moses, will remain in a future as yet undisclosed. JHWH was, is, and will be effectively present. No one has expressed this sense of promise better than the Marxist philosopher E. Bloch:

> the Exodus God...proved in the prophets his hostility to masters and to opium. Above all, he is not statically constituted like all the pagan gods before him. For the Yahweh of Moses at the very beginning gave himself a definition, a continually breathtaking definition, which makes all staticism pointless: 'God spoke to Moses: I will be who I will be.'[11]

The God of Exodus is a God who goes with the people. Present to the people, yet never limited by them, the God of the Mosaic revelation is the God of promise. Every promise must have its root in the present. Without this the promise remains insubstantial and even unintelligible. Just as JHWH is present to Moses as a hidden partner, JHWH is also disclosed as the God of the Patriarchs. From this root, but with a new promise given in Moses' experience, God's effective presence

28

is anticipated in every new disclosure. The promise already given to Abraham is both renewed and, without foreclosure on the future, made more precise.

We shall examine this promise in greater detail later. Here it must suffice to present the Name as hinting at the long pilgrimage wherein God will journey with the people. Exodus is *ex-hodos*, the way out, the pilgrimage. The name JHWH is a promise to journey on that long route. And so one must agree with those who read the enigma as 'I will be with you.' John Courtney Murray's slightly less polished translation is nonetheless appropriate: 'I shall be there, as who I am I shall be there.'[12] For accuracy and conciseness, Yves Congar's paraphrase of Exodus 3:14 is difficult to surpass:

> Who am I? My deeds will show you. I shall be what you shall see when I deliver you from Egypt, feed you in the desert, guide you to Sinai to receive my law, there to enter a covenant with me and thus become my people; I shall be the one who will punish you for your sins . . . but also the one who will deliver and re-establish you and bestow indestructible life upon you.[13]

Exodus

The exit of a motley collection of Hebrews from servitude in Egypt, commonly entitled Exodus, can be regarded in at least two ways.

The eye of the historian will discover little enough. Somewhere in the thirteenth century BC a small band of people under Pharaoh Rameses II accepted the leadership of Moses, a restless man with a developed sense of mission. Whereas Egypt had been a hospitable refuge for Jacob's many sons, a time came when welcome guests were reduced to servitude—'a Pharaoh came who knew not Joseph'. Under Moses' leadership this enslaved group, this 'Moses troop', embarked on a hazardous course of action. They confronted the monarch and, as many people have tried to do since, fled an environment which had become intolerable. After an extraordinary period of wandering, during which the effects of oppression nearly undid their resolution, they entered Canaan—according to their claim 'the promised land'. Allied to other tribes of an Israelite federation, they overcame the autochthonous inhabitants with

29

a harshness often fuelled by religious fanaticism. The subsequent history of the Exodus people was marked by a succession of tribal wars. They gained victories and suffered defeats in wars of attrition both with neighbours and with colonisers from further afield. The historian will also advert to their tenacious folk memory of a promise. This promise they interpreted in both political and religious terms. In social-religious terms the Exodus tradition is laden with religious and racial symbolism. The tradition embellishes a nucleus of fact to provide a national ideology and a relatively sophisticated theology. For later Judaism, Exodus is on the same level as the original creation. Just as in the beginning God created the world, so at the Exodus a new work of creation was afoot. The book of Isaiah interweaves God's creation at the foundation of the world and God's re-creation in the Exodus of Israel from slavery in Egypt.

The 'subversive memory' implanted in the Exodus accounts has all too frequently been tamed by rather too spiritual interpretations. Our religious traditions seem to have drawn the sting of Exodus. They confine it within purely spiritual, mystical or liturgical interpretations. J. A. T. Robinson asks if this restriction does not arise from a domestication of God.[14] A second look will show us that narrowness is here a mistake. Read from a different perspective, the Exodus account is a masterpiece in analysis of oppression and resistance. It is one of the first lessons in liberation theology, since it highlights the liberative concern of JHWH. JHWH rejects oppressive structures and practices. Having seen the sufferings of the people, JHWH takes an initiative towards their liberation. Every detail of their degradation is known to God: the forced labour, the enforced birth control, the infanticide, the manifold humiliations visited on the Hebrews. Notice the psychological realism in the resistance by the Hebrews to the call to be free: 'They did not listen to Moses; they had become impatient because of their cruel slavery' (Ex. 6:9). Over and against this injustice, JHWH takes a stand. God intervenes in history and effectively acts for the victim.

With faith in JHWH's option for an oppressed people Moses addressed the Pharaoh: 'Thus says the Lord the God of Israel; let my people go that they may hold a feast to me in the wilderness.' Moses' address is a political call for liberation. It is strategically expressed in that a modest aim is proposed (to hold a feast in the wilderness). If the Exodus succeeds in being a real way out, this is due at once to the astuteness of Moses' leadership and JHWH's efficacious action. If one reads the account from the standpoint of a commitment to human liberation, one will notice God's support for the demand for justice, and God's presence to people who act for justice. The underlying perception of Exodus is that faith in JHWH inspires the demand for fair play, that JHWH does not support sacred personages such as the Pharoah, and that concerted action by quite ordinary people can count on JHWH's effective presence. G. Guttiérrez argues that Exodus: 'desacralises social praxis which from that time on will be the work of man. By working, transforming the world, breaking out of servitude, building a just society, and assuming his destiny in history, man forges himself.'[15]

It is frequently remarked that the forty years wandering in the desert represents a journey of little more than a week or ten days. Clearly the 'forty years' is symbolic of fullness, of significance, of eventfulness. There is much to learn here about faith and perseverance, about courage and endurance, about doubt and steadfastness. Above all, there is much to learn about JHWH's particular relation to this wandering group of people. JHWH has been rightly termed the migrant God. The Moses troop is indeed a migrant community. The lesson of Exodus is that JHWH goes with them in migration. To use Yves Congar's phrase, 'where God's people is, there is God'.[16] There is a sense in which JHWH can be said to suffer with the people. Franz Rosenzweig movingly puts it: 'God gives himself away to his people, he shares in suffering its sufferings, he goes with it into the misery of exile, he shares its wanderings.'[17] Truly, then, there is a profound meaning to the text of Exodus 3:12: 'I will be with you in person'. The symbols of the divine presence are themselves evocative of pilgrimage. The cloud which accompanied the people to the threshold of the promised land is a sign of JHWH's presence, albeit in hiddenness. So, too, is the ark of covenant, moving ahead of the people to make a path for them. Again, there is the tent of meeting—surely the strongest badge of the nomadic condition of the migrants—which was placed outside the camp and where Moses could obtain divine guidance in crucial situations. Each element—cloud, ark and tent—is a reminder of JHWH's historic presence to a people in search of freedom, a measure of social justice, and religious service of a liberator God.

There were many hesitations, dissensions and recriminations. The divisive effect of oppression on the oppressed themselves has become an accepted tenet in modern social psychology. The Exodus account captures this fact very vividly as well as producing an echo of fragile loyalty: 'Were there no graves in Egypt, that you should have brought us here to die in the wilderness? See what you have done to us by bringing us out of Egypt. Is not this just what we meant when we said in Egypt, 'Leave us alone, let us be slaves to the Egyptians'? We would rather be slaves to the Egyptians than die here in the wilderness.'[18] Later there are the adoration of the golden calf and the collusion against Moses' leadership. It is as if every liberative venture is beset by discouragement and by loss of nerve. The other element which it is important to note in the Exodus literature is the subversive memory of oppression and liberation, engraved on the folk consciousness of Israel. The Torah (law) was to enjoin justice towards the weak and defenceless precisely because they, (the Hebrews) had themselves been oppressed and through JHWH's gracious action had been rescued. It has been claimed that the strongest, most enduring social criticism in the ancient world came from this heritage. A critique was fuelled by the memory of a time when Israel was subject to harsh slavery reversed only by JHWH's initiative recorded in Exodus. The memory of servitude and liberation rebounded on later selfishness and domination in Israel itself. Several impressive citations bring this out:

> Do not ill-treat or oppress a foreigner. Remember that you were foreigners in Egypt. (Exodus 22:21)

The realism of Deuteronomy 8:11-14 cannot be evaded:

> When you have all you want to eat and have built good houses to live in...make sure you do not become proud and forget the Lord your God who rescued you from Egypt when you were slaves.

The Exodus theme has become a major paradigm for every faith which aspires to transform social living. The God of Exodus is indeed the God of liberation, the God who inspires and accompanies every genuine search for fair play and justice. Even today, the Exodus paradigm guides the search for liberation. It reminds us that the God of Exodus, whose preferred name is 'I will be with you', goes with those—rather goes ahead of those—who work and suffer for liberation and justice. Yet, there is a danger of wrenching the Exodus model from the broader weave of the Old and New Testaments. Exodus cannot be isolated from related themes within Judaism. There is the earlier promise that from Abraham would come a universal healing. There is the promise that 'the land' would be given as an inheritance to Israel. There is the theme of God's dealing with humankind and of Israel's crucial role in God's purpose for all people. All this is an irreplaceable pattern, a unitary weave, although the pattern and the weave are modified by several precisions in the later books of the Old Testament. For example, Deutero-Isaiah insists that God's purposes are working in surprisingly new ways—for example, through Cyrus the Persian king and Nabuchednezzar the Assyrian tyrant.

The student of Exodus today must ask about the presuppositions at work in our reading of it. By what process do we confine ourselves to an innocuously 'liturgical' reading, as has for long been the case? On the other hand, how do we arrive at the realisation that Exodus offers a subversive memory or a point of departure for a theology of liberation? Why does one choose this theme rather than any other—e.g. exile, return, temple, covenant, creation, recreation? All these themes are prominent in both Old and New Testaments. The answer lies surely in the so-called circle of interpretation. Our present awareness of the need for liberation from unjust servitudes seeks out in the Bible corresponding affirmations for our guidance, support and encouragement. That quest is impressively met in the Exodus paradigm.

Exodus is a beacon light guiding the service of a God who refuses to underwrite oppression or enslavement. The God of Exodus stands rather with the oppressed and enslaved. The promise of freedom contained in the Exodus-memory has energised people through the centuries and does so even today. Thus, Exodus remains a powerful disclosure-symbol of God and of God's modes of action. It powerfully suggests that faith does not remain neutral in face of oppression and that God is not to be numbered in the ranks of the powerful.

Exodus is a politico-religious reality. It is not simply about political action. The Old Testament is situated within a covenanted relation of the people to God. It is to be placed against the backdrop of Jewish faith in God's work exercised in the primal creation and in the day-to-day continuance of that creative work. Because of this, Exodus must not be sundered from faith in the new creation foreshadowed in Jeremiah, Ezechiel and Isaiah. In this larger framework, God's partiality to the victim and the sufferer is seen even more clearly as part of God's purpose to bless the whole of God's creation. Nevertheless, Exodus must not be spiritualised in such a way that its powerful social critique is muted and its genuinely subversive power neutralised. The partiality of God—against oppression and for liberation—is Exodus' lasting challenge to premature calls for peace where there is no peace and for reconciliation in which a fair share of the cost has not been debited to the oppressor.

It is also true that Exodus has its shadow side. The Exodus account discloses a ruthless expropriation of other people whose land was sequestrated and whose lives were taken in the entry of the Hebrews to the 'promised land'. It is not to be overlooked that the Exodus symbol has guided projects which were later to issue in domination of yet other victims. Enda McDonagh exemplifies this succintly: 'The self-identification of North of Ireland Unionists and South African Afrikaaners has always included Exodus as part of their myth and identity, at obvious cost to North of Ireland Nationalists and South African blacks.'[19] There is, therefore, a necessity to examine critically every application of the Exodus paradigm lest a new abuse of God be set in train, lest a new group of victims be substituted for the old. As McDonagh puts it: 'Retelling the story of Exodus of Israel from Egypt is . . . a necessary but not a sufficient condition for fulfilling our liberating task.'[20]

One is pushed, therefore, to a critical understanding even of Exodus. In its regard we have to remember that its factual base, although firm, is exiguous. Hebrews did enter the Nile delta about 1800 BC. Some generations later, Pharaoh Rameses II undertook construction on a massive scale to which was conscripted prisoners, slaves, strangers—guest workers such as the Hebrews. From this servitude the Hebrews fled—a motley group under their leader Moses—and, entering a tribal confederation, managed to subdue with considerable ferocity the indigenous groupings. They were motivated by the perception that the land was promised them and that in it Yahweh could be served in righteousness and justice. Yet, in terms of world history, Exodus is insignificant. It is no more than the successful flight of a small group of Hebrews who subsequently built—by an assortment of means—a durable society.

Why, then, do we pay such attention to Exodus as a revelation of God and of God's attitudes. There is a complex of reasons. Despite its slender hold for the academic historian, Exodus has a particular density of meaning for all who are open to justice and humaneness. In a sense, this density exceeds the sum total of historical facts. The Exodus from Egypt has a surplus of meaning gained from its peculiar ability to strengthen the resolve of all who aspire to a 'way out' from oppressive situations. To say this is not equivalent to arbitrary *eisegesis* (reading into). It is an accepted hermeneutical rule that there is a surplus of meaning to every significant event which grows rather than lessens with the accumulation of its understanding and influence. Exodus is, therefore, an unfinished event. Even today it can attain new density wherever it is taken up as a paradigm for liberative search.

Inset to Exodus is a principle of auto-criticism. Without this principle even the most potent symbol of resistance, even the most firm declaration of the God of liberation, can become an *apologia* for encrusted domination. The self-criticism arises from the subversive memory of one's own servitude reversed by transformative faith in the God of justice and of re-creation. This memory contains a veto on every subsequent oppression by the erstwhile oppressed: 'Do not ill-treat or oppress a foreigner; remember that you were foreigners in Egypt' (Ex. 22:21). Here is the standard by which can be judged the perennial temptation to set up new oppressions instead of old.

35

Only if such auto-criticism (bound up with the memory of God's liberative concern for *all* oppressed people) is allowed to perdure can one hope today to practise that richer and fuller understanding of Exodus, so needed in our riven and unjust world.

3

The God of Mercy, Justice and Compassion

I

Yahweh alone is our God

The several textual strands within the first five books of the Old Testament can be identified with near exactness. Through these strands, the use of proper names for God can be traced: El, Elohim, El Shaddai, El 'Olam, Elyon and, surpassing all others in frequency and significance, the great name of Yahweh. For all this relative clarity, the circumstances in which these names emerged are lost in the nimbus of pre-testamental oral tradition.

It frequently evokes surprise that monotheism cannot be taken for granted at all points of Israel's history. The establishment of strict monotheism (Yahweh is God: there is no other) is clear from seventh century BC. In 622 BC Josiah, the king, instituted Yahweh-monotheism as a law of the state. However, many scholars argue that faith in Yahweh the one and only God, emerged from polytheism (belief in many Gods) to become first henotheism (belief in this *our* God) and finally, monotheism. The religion of Abraham, Isaac and Jacob is presented in the Old Testament much as if these were devoted Israelites of the seventh or sixth century BC. Yet, on closer attention one discerns hints of an earlier and different religious practice. At Genesis 14, Abraham is present at the worship of a Canaanite Deity which is not his God, El Shaddai. Again, Laban, with whom Jacob lived many years, is presented as having household gods which Rachel, Jacob's new wife, brought with her on her marriage.[1] The Old Testament gives ample evidence of a recurrent tendency to polytheism in the popular religion of Israel. Alongside the cult of Yahweh, lesser

37

gods of fertility, health, weather and economic gain, enjoyed a certain vogue and thus aroused the intense protest of prophetic literature. It is worth noting that archeological exploration has disclosed corroborative evidence of polytheism in the Israel of monarchic and pre-monarchic times.

The earlier books of the Old Testament—which is itself a firm record of faith in Yahweh—do not deny the existence of other gods. The book of Samuel adverts to the impossibility of worshipping God outside 'His heritage'.[2]

Even the prophet Micah can say:

> Each nation worships and obeys its own god, but we will worship and obey the Lord our God for ever and ever . . . [3]

Although too much should not be made of this late text, it could signify a henotheistic faith rather than a monotheistic one. Without subtracting from the sincerity of faith in Yahweh, questions of the non-existence of other gods are, in the main, avoided. It is as if to say: let the Assyrians worship Asher, the Egyptians Amon or Aton, the Ammonites Milcom, the Moabites Chemosh, we however will worship *our* God Yahweh. This is a practical monotheism which does not raise the theoretical distinction between henotheism and monotheism. Some commentators go so far as to suggest that while Amos and Proto-Isaiah served only Yahweh, they showed no sign of denying the existence of others' gods.

The first explicit statement of Jahwist monotheism is in the eighth-century prophet Hosea:

> I am the Lord your God who led you out of Egypt. You have no God but me. I alone am your saviour (Hos. 13:4).

Hosea vigorously contests the official temple religion with its sacrifices to the Baalim and veneration of idols (Hos. 11:2). Even earlier, in the ninth century, Elijah opposes the service of Baal and urges the worship of Yahweh-alone. King Josiah's institution of Yahwist monotheism (622) broke down shortly after his death. Yet the Yahweh-alone movement was sufficiently strong to undergird Jeremiah and Ezechiel's denunciations of going after false, non-existent gods. Both Jeremiah and Ezechiel, writing in the midst of communal breakdown, witnessed to Yahweh as the only hope of Israel.

For Jeremiah, not merely is Yahweh Israel's own God, Yahweh is the only one from whom salvation can come (2:11; 5:7). Writing a generation later, Deutero Isaiah reiterates that Yahweh is the one and only God, in comparison with whom all others are nothing. Deuteronomic history (sixth and fifth century BC) emphasises that the 'Lord is God, there is no other besides Yahweh'.[4] With this prostestation a development of almost 300 years has reached its term. Thenceforth 'Judaism possessed its monotheistic creed which it bore unaltered through history to be handed on through christianity and Islam'.[5]

The forces at work in this emergence have been the subject of speculation from many angles. Sigmund Freud in *Moses and Monotheism* derives faith in Yahweh from Egyptian worship of Aton (fourteenth century BC). However, Freud's argument is unconvincing, being little more than an extrapolation from his own views on the religious function of the father-image. Other analyses stress the political and social movements in Israel-Judah (900–600 BC). Amongst these was the Baal worship fostered in the ninth century BC by Jezebel, wife of King Ahab. Under Phoenician influence (Jezebel was from Sidon) the worship of Yahweh would have come under threat from poly-theistic cult. The subsequent accession of Jehu to the throne (and the murder of Jezebel) brought a re-alignment of foreign policy and, at home, the removal of the Baalim. There occurred an upswing in the political fortunes of those who pressed for unalloyed fealty to Yahweh. In this kind of analysis, Israel's external associations as well as internal political and religious alignments would at one time have helped and at another time have hindered the development of exclusive devotion to Yahweh.

The investigation of the rise of Yahwism as a strictly mono-theistic faith remains legitimate but highly speculative. No one can explain away the extraordinary single-mindedness of faith in Yahweh as this finds expression in the Old Testament. Without parents or offspring, without wife or consort, God is conceived of as jealous of all pretended rivals. This jealousy will not tolerate the company of deities or enter a situation of 'first among equals'. The Old Testament is dominated by the command, 'Worship no God but me' (Exodus 20:3). And so, although popular religion frequently lapsed into polytheism, although kings went after false gods for personal or political reasons, the prophetic faith of Israel stressed the exclusive service of Yahweh.

It is a salutary lesson that in the breakdown of Israel the full consistency of faith in Yahweh emerged. We are indebted to Jeremiah, Deutero Isaiah and Ezechiel for the strongest proclamation of Yahweh as the God of all people, the God who prevails even on the other side of death. This is the period when the world potential of Jewish faith comes to the fore. While remaining an Israel-centred faith, there is a universal thrust to the message it proclaims. At the low point of Israel's political fortunes a daring conceptual breakthrough is made: the 'history' of creation becomes the foreword to Israel's own troubled but ever hope-filled promise. Myth and history are conjoined to give us world history (Voegelin). Pre-existing traditions on cosmogony are joined to a reading of national-religious history. Here the universally creative power of God, the specific dealings of God with Israel and the clear delcaration of the nullity of all other 'gods' coalesce.

II

The Pattern of Old Testament Faith in God
Can one identify a pattern in the Old Testament experience of God? One attempts to do so with diffidence since the Old Testament documents a wide range of experience within the development of a people's history. Yet a pattern *can* be discerned. The Old Testament records a central perception of God which endures through all development and change. The holiness, the freedom, the transcendence of God are to the forefront of Israel's religious awareness. God is prior to every search. God seeks people out even before they have entered a quest for God. This absolute priority of God is the thrust of the opening verses of the Bible: 'In the beginning God created the heavens and the earth. . . . ' The Exodus tradition of God's liberative intervention once again details God's initative: 'I saw . . . I heard . . . I have learnt . . . I am determined . . . I sent you . . . '.[6]

With unforgettable simplicity Exodus speaks of the attributes of God. Yahweh is the one who shows compassion and pity, who is slow to anger, who is loving, faithful, steadfast, who remembers, forgives and punishes. These attributes are ingrained in biblical tradition, being repeated many times throughout the Old Testament (Pss. 86:15; 103:8; 145:8; Joel 2:13; Neh. 9:17). Behind these characteristics is the momentous avowal that God is the *living* God. Thus the reality of God is vehemently asserted—not, however, at the end of philosophical analysis or metaphysical exploration. Rather, God is known through the *ways and visitations* of self-disclosure. Burdened by the hiddenness of God, Moses asks, 'Show me thy ways, so I may know thee' (Ex. 33:13). The darkness is dispelled, the silence broken, the void filled by the ways and visitations so central to the Old Testament.

While describing God's action for and with Israel, the Old Testament does not attempt to grasp at God's inner mystery. The holiness of God, the divine transcendence of all that is not God, is entirely respected. God cannot be seen face to face: 'I will not let you see my face, because no one can see me and stay alive ... ' (Ex. 33:20).

Nevertheless, God is known through God's deeds. Through these, God's attitudes and even God's attributes can be indirectly discerned. It is not a negligible harvest. God's presence is a real presence. It yields real knowledge. Yves Congar memorably writes, 'Whenever ... God is revealed as 'the holy' at an infinite distance from us, supremely above all things, [God] is at the same time revealed as near us, turning towards us, communicating with us through a gift ... '.[7]

III

The loving kindness and mercy of God

God's presence in gift is perceived in patterns of loving kindness and faithfulness *(hesed we 'emet)*. *Hesed* connotes gracious friendliness and kindness. It is self-forgetfulness in benevolence to the other. It is the consideration which exists between host and guest (Gen. 19:19) or between sincere allies (1 Sam. 47:29). *Hesed* also means covenant love and leads to magnanimous generosity. The Old Testament recurrently celebrates the loving kindness *(hesed)* which God shows the people. God is rich in faithful kindness (Ex. 36:6-7). God keeps steadfast love to the thousandth generation. Attention has been drawn to the contrast between God's steadfast love to the thousandth generation and God's punishment which endures only to the third or fourth: '*Hesed* thus points to the abundance of grace which is richer than the necessary punishment for evil.'[8]

The rich variety in God's continuing favour emerges in several contexts. Hosea uses the image of persevering, long suffering, marital love. The fickleness of Israel's love *(hesed)* is described:

> Your love for me disappears as quickly as morning mist; it is like dew that vanishes early in the day. (Hos. 6:4)

Yahweh's *hesed* is totally different:

> I will be true and faithful
> I will show you constant love and mercy
> and make you mine forever. (Hos. 2:19)

It is tender, compassionate and merciful:

> How can I give you up O Israel?
> How can I abandon you? ...
> My heart will not let me do it,
> my love for you is too strong. (Hos. 11:8)

Here, God's loving kindness assumes the overtone of a tender, even motherly love. For Jeremiah, the patient love of God is enduring:

> My love is constant and I do what is just and right.
> (Jer. 9:24)

Deutero-Isaiah offers a moving description of this faithful love:

> The mountains and hills may crumble but my love for you will never end. (Is. 54:10)

The hesed-Yahweh is the backcloth against which God's benevolence in all its forms is placed—rescue (Ps. 109:26), redemption (Ps. 44:26), forgiveness (Ps. 25:7), mercy (Ps. 86:5). God's mercy is ever faithful. God's merciful love is thoroughly dependable. Yahweh is someone on whose words, acts and love one can rely. God is the rock of firmness, someone on whom one can rest secure. This reliability in loving kindness provides a shield and protection:

> [Yahweh's] faithfulness will protect and defend you...(Ps. 91:4)
> Lord, I know you will never stop being merciful to me, your love and loyalty will always keep me safe.(Ps. 40:11)

The grace of God (hanan) and the loving kindness of God demand a response from humankind. In the first place, the response is to go and do in like manner. Humankind cannot fully reciprocate the divine generosity. The means available do not match the divine largesse. Yet, hesed can be shown to the neighbour, the fellow human being. There is a proportionality here. As Jahweh is to us, so must we be to each other. If we have been given God's generous love, we in turn must be prepared to love one another. There is a second response. It is to give thanks and praise for God's hesed and emet. Thus, we encounter liturgical formulae in the Psalms:

> for his loving kindness abides forever (Pss. 136 and 107)

And again in 1 Chronicles:

> Give thanks to Yahweh for Yahweh is good for his loving kindness lasts forever. (1 Chron. 16:34; cf. 2 Chron. 5:13)

The very cherishing of the gifts of hesed brings to mind a tragic limit:

> Can man tell of God's loving kindness in death...(Ps. 88:11)

Bravely, the Psalmist vows, 'Your loving kindness is worth more than life itself' (Ps. 63:3). This is a brave and generous protestation. It reaches beyond the frontier of life to glimpse, although not to be behold, the limit beyond all limits—eternal life.

The Hiddenness of God

> 'A religion which does not affirm that God
> is hidden is not true.'
> *Pascal*[9]

Israel's experience of God's hiddenness is documented clearly in the Old Testament. Yahweh's involvement with the people was not always unambiguously clear. A 'dark night of the soul', for both individual and nation, forms a considerable part of the Old Testament's witness. This testimony is rendered impressive for modern-day questioning by the presence of doubt and protest at God's apparent absence. The literature of reproach and lamentation rivets attention to the rough edges of the present where exclusive attention to 'promise' could result in flight into dreaming of the future.

It has been remarked that Israel was repeatedly affected by the experience of the hiddenness of God.[10] At Exodus 17:7, the anguished question is raised: 'Is the Lord with us or not?' It is not a rhetorical question. Rather the question arises from existential fear and religious doubt. Here an answer is given—the waters of Mara gushed forth in sign that JHWH was indeed with the people. In the narrative literature this kind of question normally receives speedy answer. Gideon, the judge, asks:

> If Yahweh is with us why has all this befallen us . . . where are all his wonderful deeds which our fathers recounted?

And the answer is given:

> I will help you . . . I am sending you . . . I will stay until you come back.' (Judges 6:12; 6:14, 16, 18)

Again in the prophetic literature a singular question is raised through the experience of national disintegration. The prophets offer an answer—that the apparent absence of Jahweh is not the absence of non-being but rather a judgment on infidelity. Notice the question:

> Why is my pain increasing . . . will you be to me a deceitful stream, like water that fails . . .

The answer is given also by the prophet:

> If you return I will restore you and you shall stand before
> me...(Jer. 15:15-18).

The book of Lamentations is a moving record of a people's destruction. Here too one encounters the awareness that Yahweh has punished Israel for infidelity to the covenant. As judgment, the hiddenness of God is a void and an absence. At the close of this short book there is a heartbroken call: why have you abandoned us so long, will you remember us again?

Yet another variation of the experience of Yahweh's hiddenness is given in the Wisdom literature. This hiddenness reflects the experience of human misery (Job) and of the limited powers of human comprehension (Eccles. and Proverbs). There is puzzlement here—the weariness of pain and near scepticism devoid of all optimism. In this crucible of abandonment Job will ask 'Why do you avoid me, why do you treat me like an enemy?' (Job 13:24).

What has been termed a 'literature of dissent' is most clearly exemplified in certain psalms. These psalms address Yahweh through lament, reproach and agonised doubt. They form a large part of the book of Psalms and are well instanced by Pss. 10, 13, 27, 46, 69, 88, 89, 102.

A reproach is clear in the words of Psalm 89:

> where are the former proofs of your love?
> Where are the promises you made to David? (Ps. 89:49)

Yahweh is accused, as it were, of forgetfulness:

> Why are you hiding from us?
> Don't forget our suffering and trouble. (Ps. 44:24)

The hiddenness of God is central to the question at Psalm 88:14:

> Why do you reject me O Lord?
> Why do you turn away from me?

A variation of this anguish is expressed in yet another troubled question: How long?

> How long will your anger burn like a fire? (Ps. 89:46)

These psalms contain an immensely valuable perspective on faith itself. They show deeply felt anguish in face of personal trial and communal reverses. Their lament is primarily addressed to God from whom so much is expected. Secondarily, they describe the desperate condition of the psalmist(s) or of the people. Finally, they describe the hostile circumstances or persons that cause so much unhappiness.

Although they normally close with a renewed affirmation of faith-confidence, the weight of the lament or protest or interrogation should be recognised for itself. Without this recognition, we underestimate the significance of doubt and near despair in Israel's experience of God. Whereas in the prophetic literature a harsh but consistent explanation is given for Yahweh's seeming absence (Yahweh has judged Israel worthy of salutary punishment), in these psalms God's absence is noted but no ready explanation is given. Suffering and abandonment have come into the psalmist's life despite fidelity to God. A communal misfortune has occurred even though no guilt is evident. In a note of aggrieved despondency the psalmist challenges the hidden God. The psalmist has been falsely accused (Ps. 35:11ff.), left alone in sickness (Ps. 88:8) his God mocked (Ps. 74:9). He is not aware of infidelity to God (Ps. 44:18). Why then does God remain silent and unmindful? Will this last forever?

Claus Westermann points out that all laments in the Old Testament thrust beyond lament or petition to praise. The psalms, too, move from lament to confident praise. They are truly prayers of praise. Nevertheless, they show the reality of the struggle to attain confidence and hope: 'Without the struggle the questions directed to God would be meaningless and to interpret all questions as merely preliminary to confessions of confidence is to be indifferent to the urgency of the struggle out of which they were born.'[11] The moment of desperation must not be minimised by premature stress on the moment of praise and confidence. In these psalms we have impressive witness to that 'troubled theism' which today is part of the experience of many believing people. The experience of the silence of God, the onset of doubt and near despair, these can be truly valuable elements in the perseverance of faith. For the Old Testament, this painful moment is to be faced. Doubt and apparent despair are integral to the faith experience of Israel: 'The prayers of lament give form to even the darkest experiences and so guarantee their legitimacy in the life of faith.'[12]

The protest psalms confirm that the onslaught of doubt nigh to despair can lead to a deep, though hard-won, affirmation of faith in God's effective presence. In effect, these psalms witness to two movements. There is the experience of puzzlement, fright, and horror. Then, since the psalms are essential to the context of worship, there is a further movement deeper into a tradition which has been questioned. The disparity between the bright expectations raised by the previous favour of Yahweh, on the one hand, and the cruelly disappointing reality, on the other, is frankly admitted. God is both present and absent. God is present—how else could Yahweh be interrogated by 'How long?' and 'Why?' God is absent—how else could such cruel realities come to pass? Samuel Terrien's reference is surely apt in regard to the psalms—they display a sublimity of theological perception in discerning God's presence in absence.[13]

V

The Pilgrim God

'An evolving man can only be addressed by an evolving God.'
A. Hastings[14]

In his work *Sacred History and Humanity* (1837), Moses Hess, Zionist and Socialist, wrote of the Jews as the people 'in whom the knowledge of God became hereditary'.[15] Hess's remark is instructive for both Christian and Jewish theology. It emphasises the forcefulness of the Old Testament heritage to which both Christianity and Judaism are indebted. This complex heritage does not centre on any one 'revelation' which could then be petrified in static dogma. From one generation to another, the promise both conserves and stretches the knowledge of God in Israel. The 'wandering Jew' should be a term of respect rather than contempt. It conveys the idea of pilgrimage in the footsteps of the God of promise. In that pil-

47

grimage God is felt to be present in a manner at once hidden and yet clear, surprising and yet expected. Above all, God is experienced as supremely real. God makes the crucial difference to both personal and communal living. As individuals and in community, people are sustained by the knowledge of God. God's rule touches body and spirit. It reaches through the religious sphere, to pervade everyday living. The Old Testament discloses an extraordinary history of faithfulness despite unfaithfulness, of tenacity despite fickleness, of enduring hope despite the recurrent temptation to despair. At every point one can discern the haunting memory of the promise of God to Israel. It is this pilgrimage of faith in search of promise which can instruct our own study of the Old Testament.

The God of the promise is not any 'god' whatever. This God is a God of pilgrims. Abraham—the Father of Faith—is both nomad and pilgrim. As Deuteronomy 26 reminds us: 'a wandering Aramaean was my father...'. Abraham's way of life was nomadic. Its pattern would have been of journey and halt, halt and journey with extended family, with flock and herd. Before responding to the call to enter a pilgrimage of faith, Abraham would have worshipped a moon god who was thought to guide the caravan travelling at night in order to avoid the heat of day. Into this pattern, God (Elohim) breaks. Abraham (Abram) is called to leave his father, Terai, and his clan. With a promise of land and progeny he leaves Haran to follow God wherever he is sent. Abraham has already travelled from Ur to Haran. He settles, but God wills otherwise. God sends him further, leads him further to a foreign land which He had promised him. God makes him a nomad of faith. Thus, Abraham sets out again eventually to be shown Canaan, the promised land. At Schechem, a further precision is made. God lets Abraham see the promised land (*erets*, the very dust of the earth). Here too, the God who goes with Abraham makes a self-revelation sufficient to retain the tension between the present and the future or, better, between partial attainment and promise yet to be fulfilled.

This pattern of pilgrimage under the impulsion of a promise continues. Abraham's journey was from Ur to Haran to Canaan. He lived and died in faithful anticipation of a fulfilment he would not witness. Jacob, in whom the promise is renewed, goes from Canaan to Egypt. Moses and his troop go out from Egypt to wander for a number of years in search of the promise's fulfilment. Later, there would be forced pilgrimages to Assyria and to Babylonia. So far, the promise endures in hope, even though its terms change and the older frame of reference to territory and chosen people is almost burst assunder. Not only does the promise seem to change beyond recognition, even the very concept of God develops to a new breadth and universality. It is not accidental that the New Testament shows the theme of pilgrimage in several ways. Jesus of Nazareth goes out from Galilee. His ministry, particularly as John presents it, is directed to the centre of the promise at Jerusalem. Again, Paul's christology is a pilgrim's theology. Christ emptied himself in order to go into a far country. Thus He inherited the name which is above all names (Philippians 2:6). Paul's own wandering is extensive and sustained, from Jerusalem to Antioch and then to the Gentile world where his mission lay.

It has been remarked that promise even more than revelation preoccupies Old Testament theology. Jürgen Moltmann argues that Yahweh is not an apparitional God. Rather God is the God of promise who remains independent of sacred places and times, who remains above every manipulation through magic or myth or ritual. For Israel at its best 'the appearing of God is immediately linked with the uttering of a word of divine promise'.[16] The appearances of God to Abraham and to the later patriarchs, the theophanies of Sinai are 'the presence of an absence'.[17] The Old Testament terms for revelation are quite unsystematic. It is as if the significance of the appearances of God is not in the appearances themselves but rather in the future opened up by the promise. This awareness of divine presence-in-promise encourages the Jewish sense of history where, although past and present are important, the future is of major significance for the knowledge and service of God.

What does it mean to say that God's self-disclosure is by way of promise rather than ephiphany. Does it mean a vague agnosticism, the affirmation of a God of yesterday and tomorrow but never of today? Surely not. It is to say that God's disclosure transcends both appearances (ephiphany) and the propositions which interpret appearance (dogma). The promise given and renewed discloses God as 'the future in every present'. To attend only to the present is to make absolute the *status quo*. Thus a divine sanction is given to an inhuman 'now' and the transformative intent of God is masked. God becomes linked to myth and magic, to sacred times and places and rituals. This is the crippling effect of every attempt to trammel or domesticate God. The divine transcendence is made trivial. Human effort is absolved of responsibility for being the active subject rather than passive object of history. With its emphasis on promise, the Old Testament respects God's freedom and remains open to the transformative pull of the future.

The earlier books of the Old Testament disclose the idea of a God who goes with the people, who opens up possibilities and responsibilities for the future. There is, therefore, a balance of present and future, of givenness and absence. On the one hand, the idea of effective presence is strong. On the other hand, when the people, now settled down to agrarian pursuits, are tempted to bind God to human prediction, their presumption is denied in the name of the promise. Moltmann remarks that 'the Israelites took the wilderness God of promise with them...[when they] endeavoured to master the new experiences in the land in the light of the God of promise'.[18] With the gift of the land the further requirements of consolidation as God's people open up. And so the promise is seen to include prosperity in the land and duration in the enjoyment of it. The continuation of negative experiences such as hunger, thirst, disease and harassment, sharpens the need for Yahweh's further gift of guidance, preservation and blessing.

This was not a smooth achievement. When the Israelites settled the land and became a largely agrarian people they moved towards the institution of a kingship, a temple and a priesthood. Temple normally represents a settled religion rather than the pilgrimage of faith. The temple symbolises heaven on earth, a sacred precinct in which to encounter the sacred. There the threatening present is forsaken for a timeless space of encounter. All too easily, Israel could forget that Yahweh comes in promise or in a kind of absence. The prophets of the eighth and seventh centuries—Amos,

Malachai and Jeremiah—reminded the people that God is not captured by any earthly kingship or imprisoned in any earthly temple. The glory of God may indwell the temple but never in a predictable way. To do the truth, to institute justice, to practise faithfulness, these bring one closer to true knowledge of God than institutions, rites and practices.

Thanks to the witness of the great prophets, each partial fulfilment of promise opens up an even wider vista for fulfilment. The Jewish people were not permitted the melancholy of fulfilment.[19] The destruction of the temple and the dispersal of the people were interpreted by Jeremiah as a judgment on the lack of due reverence. It was a judgment for the neglect of justice and also for presumption. The shame of dynastic history—the exaction and multiple infidelities of the kings—had drawn the judgment of God. It was a judgment which was the obverse side of the promise. Even here, however, the promise is not made null and void. Yahweh's faithfulness is verified even in judgment.

In the seventh and sixth centuries BC Israel seemed in process of disintegration as a nation. Its kingship was crushed. Its temple was ruined. Its priesthood was degraded. This ruin is interpreted as divine judgment upon unfaithfulness. The promise is now seen to go from the particularism of earlier times where JHWH was the God of *this* people, the giver of *this* land. Disappointment at the failure to live up to the promise made Amos rock the confident arrogance of Israel:

'Are you Israelites not like Cushites to me?'
says the Lord.
'Did I not bring Israel up out of Egypt,
the Philistines from Caphtor,
the Aramaeans from Kir?' (Amos 9:7)

With the Babylonian exile and the rise of Isaian prophecy the universal purpose of God is discerned. Yahweh, the God of Israel, is the God of all people. The promise of God is neither reneged upon nor withdrawn. Rather it is widened to embrace a universal kingdom of justice, love and peace. The second Isaiah articulates the misgiving:

'The Lord has abandoned us. He has forgotten us' (Is. 49:14).

51

The preliminary answer is a consoling one. The promise is not negated:

> Even if a mother should forget her child I will never forget you. (Is. 49:15)

Yet, Deutero-Isaiah achieves a radical transposition of thought. The centrality of Israel is modified by a much broader look upon the meaning of God's promise. God is the God of the nations, the creator of all. God can work even through the hated Nabuchednezzar (Jeremiah) and through the liberal Cyrus (Deutero-Isaiah). The idea of a compassionate God, even of a suffering God, emerges. God is hungry for justice and wholeness among all people. In the humiliation of Israel a new vision of God emerges. God's salvation will extend to the ends of the earth: God's justice will shine on the nations. A day of Yahweh will dawn out of the present night of judgment. This new departure is expressed in images taken from Israel's history. These images speak of a new covenant, a new Exodus, a new Zion, a new land. Central to Deutero-Isaiah's vision is the suffering servant of God. This theme is heavy with significance for Christian theology. It gives a new and very powerful insight into how God deals with us. From the tribulation of the exile, the prophet's witness extends the understanding of the Abrahamic promise to its outer limits. Salvation is for all. It is for Israel certainly, but through Israel it is for all. Here the missionary task emerges. Israel is called to be a light to the nations of the known world.

Not only is the extent of the promise seen to be universal, the content of the promise is viewed more exactly. Earlier, the ideas of land, people, prosperity and special closeness to God formed the contours of the promise. In the prophetic literature, one finds a new depth in these same hopes. Now, divine forgiveness, removal of oppression, relief of hunger and poverty, the commencement of a universal peace, move into prominence. A perspective is opened up in which the question of the conquest of death is raised. One does not find an explicit treatment of resurrection, immortality or survival after death. Yet, it is asserted that the dead will share the promise and the glory. Death itself is capable of being transformed through the power of one who is Lord both of the living and the dead. In this way the horizon of promise is seen to extend even beyond the boundary of death.

VI

The God of the Kingdom

The kingdom of God (the reign of God or the kingdom of heaven) is central to Old Testament expectation. In face of defeat the expectation of a kingdom of God kept hope alive. The kingdom of God was a symbol that things could be otherwise. The idea of the kingdom knitted into the expectation of an original promise made to Abraham and thereafter developed in the people's memory. The kingdom of God, therefore, forms part of the Utopian expectation of Jewish faith, an expectation which served to unsettle every unworthy settlement or inhumane establishment.

The concept of God's kingship predates Israel's own institution of a human king. Already, the Exodus tradition speaks of Yahweh as Lord and King: 'You Lord will be King forever and ever' (Exodus 15:18). This kingship does not map out a geographic unit nor does it speak of a directly political reality. The kingdom of God is the saving action of God. It is a present reality in so far as the very existence of the people is an evidence of God's Lordship. Wherever the law of God is observed or the first commandment prayed there the kingdom of God is at work. On the other hand, the kingdom has yet to be attained. It is a future reality, something yet to come. Nowhere is the disparity between actuality and ideal more clearly recognised than in Judaism. There is little danger that the present time, with its insecurity and its threat, will be mistaken for the kingdom. Even if Yahweh's mighty acts in favour of Israel are interpreted as evidence of God's reign, the institution of the kingdom is normally viewed as a coming reality. It *will* come at a future time and in the day of the Lord.

The blessings of the coming kingdom reflect Israel's concept of God. The expectation of the kingdom is itself a powerful, if indirect, theology of God. The kingdom will be a universal kingdom. For God is king not simply of Israel but of all people. The kingdom will be a kingdom of salvation bringing wholeness, healing, exhilaration. For God is the God of wholeness and of joy. Again, the kingdom will be a kingdom of peace, justice and liberation. For God is the God of peace, of justice, of liberation. The kingdom will bring overflowing bounty. For God is the God of overflowing bounty:

> When he is king, the people of Judea will be safe
> and the people of Israel will live in peace.
> He will be called *the Lord our salvation.* (Jer. 23:6)

It would be unrealistic to omit the recurrent attempts to harness the kingship idea to specific projects: material wealth, the restoration of David's kingship, the creation of a world-wide Jewish state, the expulsion of Roman invaders. It is not within the purpose of this study to trace the many kinds of messianism which attempted a premature foreclosure on what was God's secret. The coming kingdom, in its full inauguration, will be at a time known only to God. In the Christian view the many attempts to grasp at a premature realisation of the promised future fell far short of the suffering form in which the new realisation of the kingdom came to pass.

4

The Humanity of God

I

FOR the Old Testament God goes with the people. This active presence is a testing presence. It brings consolation, strength and hope. To speak only of 'the cruel God of the Jews' is grossly misleading.[1] It misrepresents the Old Testament as well as the subsequent history of Judaism. Faith in God's presence takes many shapes in the Old Testament. It evokes diverse moods and responses. Yahweh is neither uniformly harsh nor absent nor arbitrary. Yahweh is the God of life, of joy and of grace.

And yet, the Christian affirmation insists that the goodness and humanity of God (*benignitas et humanitas Dei*) fully appear only in Jesus the Christ, the Son of the living God. The Gospel according to John affirms 'no-one has ever seen God, the only Son . . . has made Him known'.[2] God had always been known warmly, reverently, existentially. Yet, it was knowledge from behind. God could not be seen face to face. No-one could see God and live. Far from bringing death, to see God in Christ brings life and healing. The names of Jesus—Immanuel and Jehosua—emphasise this blessed presence.[3] Here God showed God's true countenance. What does this mean? It means that our manner of relationship to God takes on a new character. Christ is the sacrament of encounter with God: 'to meet Jesus is to encounter God'.[4]

In speaking of the originality of Jesus, one has to observe a due caution. Respect is owed to the background from which Jesus came as a person and as a teacher. Religiously and socially he was a Jew. His religious consciousness related to the law and the prophets. His religious practice centred on the synagogue and the temple. While these did not circumscribe his extra-ordinary authoritativeness they represented the flavour of his speech and his thought. In this sense, it is true to say that 'Jesus did not found a church, (rather) he found one'.[5]

Again, if one believes that the great deeds of God reach a climax in the person and work of Jesus, one must nonetheless avoid depreciation of the humanity of Jesus and the everyday—even hidden—quality of his work. In the gradual disclosure of his significance the full reaches of what he has to tell us about God are shown forth. For this very reason the preference of much theological writing today is to follow a low-ascending christology even where the central focus is Christ as the disclosure of the 'pilgrim God for a pilgrim people'.

Paul reminds us that the cross of Jesus is scandal to the Jews and folly to the Gentiles. This varied perception brings home how new, surprising and disturbing were Jesus' person and work in the context of the revelation of God. If one accepts that God was in Christ reconciling the world unto God, one has to ponder the unprecedented humility of God's disclosure. The New Testament grapples with this in several ways. Paul's text, just cited, is one such way. Another attempt to express the approach of God in Jesus is the idea of *kenosis*. This is the self-emptying whereby divinity was not jealously guarded. Rather an Exodus was made—a way of suffering was entered. If this is taken at all seriously, we must look again at Jesus' 'days of the flesh' when he lived, taught, healed, suffered and died. What has this pattern of action to tell us about God the Pilgrim?

In the first place we must ask how much can we know of the historical Jesus. Here, we have to live with a modicum of relativity.[6] The gospels are not biographies. From beginning to end they present a portrait of Jesus of Nazareth perceived in the eye of faith. Thus, we can never short circuit the gospels to get at the words and deeds of Jesus 'in themselves'. That is not to say we are given a false slant or that we must limit ourselves to a Christ of faith, totally dissociated from the Jesus of history. The New Testament — through its particular perspective and along its several avenues of approach—intro-duces us to Jesus of Nazareth. There is a body of words and actions which can confidently be predicated of the historical

56

Jesus. In Jesus we have to deal not with a creation of faith unrelated to history but with someone attested to by witnesses whose faith is rooted firmly in his total history. For an ascending christology it is not necessary that we can identify a large number of words and deeds 'in themselves'. It *is* necessary that we can assume the substantial accuracy of the picture presented of Jesus in the gospel texts.

To argue thus is to call in question one of the great dogmas formulated by a line of thinkers from Reimarus to Bultmann. For these, there is a radical split between faith and history. A practical consequence is that the Christ of faith is sundered from the Jesus of history. Yet it can be argued that the faith-history dichotomy is merely another version of the spirit-body duality.[7] Just as the division of soul and body is an inadequate view of the person, so too the sundering of faith and history does less than justice to the way of being human that faith and history together represent. This is not to underestimate the delicacy of the task of identifying 'the perspectival image or memory impression' of Jesus contained in the New Testament. It is not to deny that we have to live with a 'certain relativism'. It is not to ignore that today's agreement may be tomorrow's disagreement about what was said or done by Jesus himself. Rather it is to place an act of confidence in the exercise of historical imagination working within a community or tradition of faith as it confronts a written record of the foundation of that tradition.

II

God as Abba, Father

'Father', comes from Jesus' own lips. With some exceptions, even the most exigent critics allow that it is one of his *ipsissima verba*. Its use is ascribed to him some 170 times in the New Testament. The strands of tradition in the gospels show that Jesus invariably addressed God as *my father*.[8] In these traditions there are 16 separate contexts where the 'Father' address is used by Jesus. At Mark 14:36, the Aramaic form is preserved even in the Greek version: 'Abba, father: All things are possible for you. Take this cup of suffering away from me. Yet, not what I want, but what you want.' This usage influenced Christian communities as far flung as Galatia and Rome in their address Abba, father. Jesus' prayer-address to Abba became universal in the Church, thus going far beyond the communities of purely Jewish origin (cf. Rom. 8:15; Gal. 4:6).

It is commonplace to stress that Abba means father or little father. In the close familiar relationships of Jewish society, it was an intimate, child-like address from children to father. By Jesus' time it had come to be used in a more adult honorific sense. Respected elders could be addressed as Abba. In every instance the address connotes love, respect, and a degree of intimacy. Because of this overtone of familiarity, the designation was very sparingly used of God. And as a direct address it was never so used.

The social and religious prescriptions of Judaism were coloured by a strong paternalism. It is not really surprising that in common with neighbouring cultures Judaism conceived of God in paternalist terms. In Old Testament times God was called father: father of the King; father of Israel; father of the People. Nonetheless, the older strands of Judaism rarely used the title 'father'. Invariably, qualifiers were inserted to safeguard the divine mystery and transcendence. In saying this, one does not take from the beauty and high theological content of texts like Jeremiah 31:20; Isaiah 63:16; 2 Samuel 7:14.[9]

Jesus, however, represents a totally new departure.[10] The striking thing is not so much that he called God 'father'. More significant is the direct, familiar, intimate address he employs. Here, the traditional qualifiers of respect (father of heaven and earth) or of function (father of the king or of the nation) are not employed. Jesus goes beyond similes and metaphors. His relation with his father is expressed directly, intimately and familiarly. In all the writings of Judaism there is no example of the use of Abba as a direct address to God whether in public liturgy or private prayer. This mode of address seems to be the prerogative of Jesus of Nazareth.[11]

Jesus used the term Abba at three levels of intimacy. When praying or alluding to his own relation to the father he used 'my father'. In speaking to his followers about God as compassionate and loving, as one who is suitably addressed in prayer, he used the term 'your father'. In speaking of his own message when under hostile pressure he referred to 'the father'.[12] In all cases the overtone of filial love is strong. So too is the re-echo of reverence. When Jesus forbids his disciples to call anyone 'father', it is precisely as a matter of respectful intimacy and of intimate respect for the Father who is God.

What, then, does Abba on the lips of Jesus tell us about the God to whom he so intimately related? Doubtless, we must start with the current understanding of father. We must assume that while stretching its meaning Jesus would nonetheless have taken into account such current understanding. In a patriarchal society the notion of paternal authority would have counted for a great deal. Within the family the father's authority was virtually unquestionable. It overrode any authority or autonomy on the part of wife or children. On the other hand, the father was responsible for teaching his sons(!) the law and the customs of religion. He was also to teach the secrets of his trade or avocation. Hence, when Jesus speaks of doing the will of the father (Mk. 14:16) he stands well within the traditions of Jewish society. It is likewise with 'the parable within a parable': 'Father, Lord of heaven and earth, I thank you because you have shown to the unlearned what you have hidden from the wise and learned' (Matt. 11:25-27). The authority with which Jesus witnesses to the Father resides in the full communication made by the Father to him.

Doubtless, the strong paternalism of such family life is to us strange and even oppressive. Accepting partnership in the family, we are shocked by the authoritarian and anti-female bias of the patriarchy. It is all the more necessary to note that Jesus breaks the bounds of any narrow conception of fatherhood. The positive, nutritive aspects of God's fatherhood are taken up by him recurrently: 'be ye compassionate as your heavenly father is compassionate' (Luke 6:36). The universal concern of God for all is stressed—for the good and the bad, the just and the unjust. The parable of the prodigal son, or perhaps the prodigal father, touches the right note. Here God's fatherhood means joyous acceptance, without care for merits, when the prodigal freely returns.

The Abba experience of Jesus is the basis of his words and

actions. However, that experience is not directly available to us. We have to depend on the pattern of Jesus' ministry for the clue to understanding his constant address to his Father. Together, the word and the practice of Jesus enable us to see a new way of walking with God. Jesus' whole ministry raises the question of God in a way continuous with the Old Testament, yet startlingly new in its humaneness, liberality, compassion and freedom. Jesus mirrored the inclination of his people to seek out God's will in everything. However, as distinct from the prevailing tendency towards élitism, harshness and formalism, Jesus insisted upon God's merciful rule. The God of Jesus is a God bent upon the well-being of humanity. Jesus' call for conversion was for a turning again to God in service of the least of the brotherhood/sisterhood. Later, the followers of Jesus correctly saw that he embodied the coming rule of God. They came to believe that through him we too can have the courage to call God 'Father'. The condition of that privilege is that we endeavour to serve, after the manner of Jesus, the coming of the Father's kingdom.

Far from presenting an alienating conception of God, Jesus preached a God whose concern was the good of humankind. The God of Jesus of Nazareth is the loving father concerned for and lovingly present to the most humble inhabitant of creation. In his rejection of all oppression whether religious or political, Jesus showed himself sensitive to the history of suffering. This is a history of violence towards the weak and of enslavement of the poor. In contesting such violence Jesus called on God as the one who is solicitous for the sufferer, who refuses to allow the murderer to go scot-free. Despite surrounding threat, Jesus insists that God is Abba who gives a future to those who humanly speaking have no future. In doing so, Jesus takes up the best of the Old Testament witness. The tradition from Exodus to Deutero-Isaiah proclaims that God is God of justice and of solidarity with the sufferer. The originality of Jesus is to concentrate such faith and hope under the new symbol of Abba. Whereas a run-down tradition insisted on a sectarian, legalistic God, favourable only to those who observed the *minutiae* of the Law, Jesus pointed to a God whose care endured through life and death, through good fortune and bad. His Abba touched lightly the sinner, received back the prodigal, and cherished the weak.

Thus we can best understand the Lord's prayer. In giving it to his disciples, Jesus followed a long-standing tradition among teachers in Israel. This simple, direct, life-related prayer is suitable to the way of life of Jesus and his band of followers. Theirs was an itinerant situation. The Our Father evidences the experiences of wandering, close fellowship, strains and tensions as well as ultimate trust in a present father. The similarities between Jesus' prayer and the Kaddish (an Aramaic prayer used at the end of the sermon in the Synagogue) have been noted. The Kaddish runs:

> Glorified and sanctified be his great name in the world which he created according to his will. May his kingdom come in your lifetime and in your days, and in the lifetime of the whole house of Israel, soon and without delay. And to this say: Amen.

J. Jeremias reconstitutes the original Lord's Prayer thus:

> Dear Father,
> May your name be hallowed,
> May your kingdom come,
> Give us today our bread for tomorrow
> And forgive us our debts,
> As we also, herewith, forgive our debtors,
> And let us not fall into temptation.[13]

Here indeed is an empowerment and a privilege. The traditional introduction to the Lord's Prayer conveys the sense of privilege in addressing God as Father. We dare to call God our Father—*audemus dicere.* Equivalently, our common daughterhood/sonship is declared.

III

The Kingdom of God

For too long, theology has negelcted Jesus' powerful disclosure of the reign or kingdom of God. This is a paradoxical omission for the kingdom of God is central to the words and actions of Jesus. The term *Basileia tou theou* (kingdom of God) recurs in Mark and Luke. It is the vividly descriptive title Jesus gave to the cause for which he lived and died. As with Abba, biblical criticism traces the term to Jesus himself. It lies at the heart of his work. It is at the core of his preaching.

As we have seen, the 'reign of God' is by no means foreign to the Old Testament. It is not about territorial rule. Rather, it is God's intervention on behalf of God's people. God's reign (*malk-uta*) shows itself in unprogrammed freedom. It is always gift, always gratuitous love. It is manifested in the protection of the weak, the poor, the widow and the orphan. The kingdom is nothing other than the dynamic rule of God.[14] At the time of Jesus God's rule was awaited by the Zealots, the Pharisees, the Essenes and the Sadducees. These parties lived in tension with each other. The Zealots' life-project was to bring about God's rule. They conceived of that rule in predominantly religio-political terms. Fiercely zealous for the Torah (law) they hated the Roman occupier. In consequence—surely with justification—they were critical of every collaboration with the *Imperium.* Thus, they confronted not only the Roman establishment but also the Jewish religio-political leadership which they despised as a venal compromise. With consistent heroism, the Zealots endured torture and execution. Through several generations they went to their deaths unbowed. After AD 66 they made a last stand at the inner temple, expecting God's intervention to inaugurate the kingdom.

In a different way, the Essene community at Qumran awaited the same kingdom. Rejecting the corruption at Jerusalem, the Essenes withdrew to enclaves in the desert. There they lived in ascetic preparation for the coming kingdom. The Pharisees followed yet another programme. Looking to the temple, they tried to extend ritual purity and doctrinal orthodoxy to the minutest details of everyday living. In their regard, the gospel is marked by a polemic dating from after Jesus' time. Nonetheless it seems clear that at the time of Jesus the Pharisees' aspiration to foster the service of God had deteriorated to a harsh legalism. This legalism earned Jesus' trenchant criticism for its repressive attitudes to the weak.

Finally, the Sadducees—conservative and aristocratic—collaborated with foreign occupation in the way typical of all oligarchies. More than the Pharisees they had brought the service of God down to the level of self-seeking pragmatism: 'As long as tithes were being paid and the ceremonial liturgy of the temple carried out, they saw no reason to doubt that God was sovereign of the land even if the Romans had political control over it.'[15]

There is a sharp, almost brusque clarity in Jesus' announcement: 'Repent and be converted, the kingdom of God is amongst you.'[16] It is as if 'zero hour' has arrived with its urgent demand for a radical change. Jesus declares the kingdom of God 'in the midst'. It is at the doors. It commences here and now. The kingdom heralded by Jesus is no mere psychological condition. Nor is it simply an affair of the inner heart. A sense of urgency, almost of alarm, pervades the injunction 'repent and be converted'. The kingdom of God is no luxury item or optional extra. It is a matter of life or death.

The coming of the kingdom is never described by Jesus. He offers no timescale. Rather he says, 'Of that hour no-one knows, not even the son but only the father.' Jesus did not outline a detailed strategy of the kingdom's inauguration. Instead, he held out a fresh possibility for walking in God's presence. He exemplified a new way of living in the sight of God and in true sisterhood/brotherhood. Rather than a detailed programme he offered hints of unsuspected possibilities for people oppressed by formalism and legalism. Above all else, the kingdom is announced as good news. It is a tiding of hope, a promise of joy. Jesus' preaching is an *evangelion* or good news. Whereas John preached imminent judgment, Jesus opened up a broader alternative. He presented the reign of God as marked by kindness, forgiveness and faith. This was nothing less than a new relationship to God. The God of Jesus is a God of joy, of uplift, of gratuitous love. So he preached. So he practised. For diverse kinds of people—James and John, Matthew, the woman from whom many devils were driven out, Zaccheus—the announcement of the kingdom meant a new, attractive and transformative way of life. Even more, it heralded a new encounter with God. It brought a fresh presentation of God's 'face'. The kingdom announced by Jesus is nothing other than the unconditioned and free grace of God meeting us in our concrete situations and contexts.

Jesus put new wine into old wineskins. While using the relatively familiar idea of God's kingdom he radically redefined it. He re-cast the conception of God and of God's attitudes. The very people hitherto excluded in the name of God—the menial, the excommunicated, the unholy—were the immediate beneficiaries of his ministry. So, too, were the suffering, the poor and the lonely. These Jesus declared to be the inheritors of the kingdom: blessed are you poor for yours is the kingdom of heaven. When, in various ways, the blind, the crippled, the deaf and dumb, the tax collectors and the prostitutes were touched by Jesus, they were also encountering the kingdom of God. The healing and rehabilitation brought by Jesus were earnests of the kingdom: 'If I by the finger of God drive out the devils, be sure that the kingdom of God has come upon you.'[17] Jesus' acts of mercy and of healing are indeed 'the wonderful works of God' (*magnalia Dei*). However, they are neither 'stunts' nor 'coups' in our modern sense. Jesus refused to be cast as a wonder-worker. When he healed those broken in mind or body it was always as a sign of something greater. His response to human need announced God's presence. The healing acts of Jesus are a signal in both negative and positive senses. In the negative sense, they signal that the demonic powers—those chaotic opponents of the creativity of God—are being repelled. In the positive sense, the blessedness he brought into many lives exemplifies God's concern for humankind. When Jesus invites the hitherto excluded, when he blesses the poor, the humble and the despised, when he casts out fear, when he institutes rejoicing, he declares what God is like more clearly then many treatises. God is indeed the God of mercy, of joy, of hope, of gladness. Of this, the practice of Jesus is the most powerful evidence.

In the gospels, the forgiveness of sins is a particularly strong evidence of God's presence. By God's power the sinner is reconciled with God, with others and with self. That reconciling power is mediated through Jesus. He showed a light touch with the repentant sinner. Neither condemnation nor reproof enters his conversation with even the most public sinner: 'Has no man condemned thee, neither do I condemn thee.' It was not the sinful past which preoccupied Jesus. The important thing is rather reconciliation and rehabilitation of the sinner. The joy released by conversion is a dominant emphasis. So too is God's loving acceptance of the sinner. The major role is given to the liberation rather than to the sin. When challenged about the sinners he befriends, Jesus refuses to apologies. Edward Schillebeeckx observes that 'crucial to his understanding of God's lordship is his utter indifference to the sinful past of another person'.[18] Little wonder that his announcement of this kind of kingdom is bitterly resisted by the complacent and the self-righteous.

An element notable in Jesus' practice is the openness with which he received all kinds of people. His relationship to women seems far more accepting and open than even the most advanced of that time. His followers included many women. To the dismay of his disciples, he conversed alone with the woman of Samaria. Women figure in his parables just as do men. In distinction from accepted custom Jesus treats women in terms of equality. For him they are normal members of society, neither more nor less. They are truly part of the kingdom of God.

The motley composition of the twelve—Matthew, the civil servant, Simon the Zealot, the gentle John and the impetuous Peter—shows Jesus' concern for inclusiveness rather than exclusiveness. The people with whom he ate or with whom he consorted form a broad range. And so he was accused of eating with publicans and sinners. The conviviality of Jesus was in fact a parable of the kingdom of God. It embraced those normally excluded or omitted. It favoured these, rather than others who might be presumed to occupy the places of honour as of right. Jesus' challenge overturns the normal hierarchies of favour: 'When you give a feast do not invite those who will invite you, but invite the lame, the halt, the maimed, and those from whom you will not have an invitation.'[19] Immense joy is brought by Jesus to people of little account in the normal reckoning. His friendship with the marginal and the forgotten overturns the usual relationships of patronage and favour. It subverts the all too frequent preferences based upon prestige, success and wealth.

What emerges from this pattern? In preaching the kingdom and in instituting anticipations of its coming, Jesus places human relationships in a new light. Relationship with God.

Relationships with other people. These were to be defined by service rather than domination, by sharing rather than selfishness, by radical equality rather than oppressive hierarchy. Kingship was no longer to be an exercise of domination. It was to be about service and compassion. Little wonder that Matthew would formulate it, 'You know that the princes of this world exercise authority over them but, with you it shall not be so.'[20] Here lies the radicalness of Jesus. The relationships he proposes subvert the cruelties of earthly power. They overturn the presumption that masters should be over slaves, that men should dominate women (or vice versa), that white should prevail over black (or vice versa), that rich should precede poor. This insistence upon equality in the sight of God, this persistence in bringing grace-filled interaction between people, threatens congealed patterns of domination.

Jesus spoke to people as individuals, not as members of a crowd. His announcement of God's kingdom touched persons, not collectivities. The kingdom is about the well-being of inidvidual men and women and children. Persons, not groups, are forgiven. Persons, not groups, become converted. Persons experience the joy of being touched by the finger of God in Jesus. The kingdom of God is in this sense intensely personal. Again, the kingdom of God is religious. It establishes a new relationship to God. The kingdom is where God's name is honoured in people's minds and hearts, in their words and deeds. To say that the kingdom of God is only about groups would misrepresent the very thing in which Jesus far outstripped all others—His full attention to persons as persons. And so, one must emphasise that the kingdom of God—and, indeed, the God of the kingdom—addresses people in their personal and religious lives.

However, one must say more. Jesus stands well within his Jewish tradition. He challenged it radically without over-turning it. The Jewish tradition laid a major stress upon the individual as part of the 'people'. Jesus came from such a background and did not repudiate it. The kingdom of God would have had for him the social and political dimension which faith in God had for all his people. To overlook this would ignore an important element in Jesus' presentation of both the kingdom of God and the God of the kingdom.

Jesus' announcement of the kingdom of God has social and political overtones. He carried out a critique of power—of Herod, of Scribes and Pharisees, of Pilate. He presented an alternative vision of social order where the first will be last and the last first. Age-old, repressive and cruel ways are contested. New forces are released. If the blind see, if the lame walk, if the poor are conscious that God loves them with preference, then things can never again be quite the same. It is certain that the various establishments saw this clearly. They recognised that Jesus' practice was dangerously subversive.

Is the kingdom *now* or in the future? One can say—since Jesus said it—that the kingdom of God is 'in the midst'. It is *now*. It is wherever healing, wholeness and joy are instituted by Jesus: 'Today this scripture is being fulfilled in your hearing.'[21] On the other hand, these blessings are anticipations rather than fulfilment of the kingdom promise. Jesus also speaks of the *coming* kingdom. His references to it are in future tense as well as in present. Along with the promise of the kingdom Jesus spoke of an impending threat. This is the great trial from which, in the Our Father, he teaches us to pray deliverance. Although he thought and acted as a prophet, Jesus shared with the Apocalyptists an awareness of the last days wherein new choices and new ways are called forth. The great trial (*peirasmos*) discloses an appalling alternative to the kingdom for which Jesus labours.

Hence, it must be said that Jesus presented the kingdom of God without precision of timescale. The kingdom retains the open-endedness of a powerful symbol of hope, urgency and effort. There is, for us, a tension between the 'now' and the 'not yet'. This tension reminds us that the kingdom is in the making. It comes today wherever the just, the healing, the liberative thing is done. Leonardo Boff puts it well: 'Whenever anyone does the will of God, it is not only for the person but also for the world that the kingdom of God comes.'[22] The kingdom is repelled wherever there is injustice or inhumaneness. In any event the definitive coming of the kingdom is not in human power. Over every human attainment in the service of God there lies a surplus of expectation. We are reminded that the making of history is not totally in our hands. In the last analysis, the subject of history is God and not man/woman, even though every man and woman without exception becomes part of the ultimate meaning of history.

IV

The Parables of Jesus

That Jesus spoke in parables is underlined by the gospels. It is also an assured fact of biblical criticism. Much has been written of the parables in Jesus' pattern of work. Many theologians speak of Jesus as *the parable of God's revelation.* How far does attention to the parables in the ministry of Jesus, and to Jesus as the parable of God, take us in contemporary knowledge and service of God?

Parabolic discourse was not specific to Jesus. It was part of the stock in trade of teachers of wisdom in the Semitic culture. However, the use of parable was as closely associated with Jesus' ministry as were his healing actions and meals with his followers. They were at the centre of his dealings with people. Inseparably linked to the announcement of God's kingdom, they confront us with patterns of actions in the spirit of the kingdom of God. Likewise, they offer insight not so much into the inner nature of God as into God's attitudes to people in the circumstances of their everyday lives. Critical scholarship insists that it is not possible to reconstruct the precise situations which evoked each parable. It appears that the greater number of parables have undergone reconstruction at the hands of one, two or three generations of the followers of Jesus. Yet several clues lead us to divine the novel and disturbing contexts of their original use. 'Tax collectors and sinners' of all kinds kept coming to hear him. The Pharisees and the Scribes grumbled about this fact. Immediately there follows the parable of the lost sheep and of the lost coin (Luke 15:1-10). Clearly, the parables were part of the good news for the poor and the outcast. They announce that God loves the poor and despised, cares about them and seeks them out with special diligence.

In their original context the parables were probably 'open-ended'. They did not necessarily finish with the specific lesson that the evangelists may have imposed on them. The overall

68

thrust of the parables is that God's cause is the cause of humankind. Some parables allude to the coming of God's kingdom. It is a gradual process of maturation (parable of the mustard seed), admission to it is not by prescription of birth or race or presumptuous expectation (parable of the uninvited guests). Other parables evoke a pattern of action in the spirit of the kingdom—seriousness and alertness in responding to the kingdom's challenge (pearl in the field; the wise virgins), true brotherhood/sisterhood (the good Samaritan). Yet others point to the mercy and generosity of God (Luke 18:10-14; 18:7), to the comfort generously afforded by God (Luke 16:19-31), to the divine magnaminity (Matt. 18:23; 20:1-16; Luke 15), to the long suffering patience of God (Luke 13:6-9; 13:24-30). Finally, there are parables which give an insight into the attitudes of God. The one which immediately comes to mind is the 'prodigal father'. The generosity of God is evoked by the long-suffering patience of this father. Again, the concern of God for every person is pointed up by the parable of the earthly father who feeds his children with true nourishment and not with a serpent or a stone.

The parable is a teaser. It gets people to think for themselves. It energises the hearer to go further in the direction to which she or he is pointed. Parables start the process of thinking for oneself—'a parable is meant to start the listener thinking by means of a built-in element of the 'surprising' and the 'alienating' in a common everyday event.'[23] Paul Ricoeur argues that the parable moves through orientation, disorientation and reorientation. Having taken for granted a common world of discourse, the parable carries the listener in a particular direction (orientation). It then brings the listener up against the hard edge of disturbance through a shock element. Here, there is disorientation from the usual, the commonplace, the accepted. From this, one is perhaps driven in a totally new direction (reorientation). Frequently the parable presents two ways of living. One is the conventional non-challenging way while the other is the exciting way of the coming kingdom.

It has been remarked that Jesus' parables are secular. Their situation is an everyday mundane one rather than anything religious or sacred. They do not point us out of the world.

Rather they show new possibilities within the world. If the possibilities are *within* this world, they are also *new* possibilities. They disclose a way of living, thinking and relating to people greatly different from the *status quo*. They overturn the traditional hierarchies, assumptions and dualisms. Again, the parables of Jesus are indirect. With three exceptions they speak of God indirectly.[24] Directly they speak of everyday realities or situations. Indirectly they move beyond the everyday and the commonplace. They contain within them a trigger point which can impel a move from the everyday to the extraordinary. The 'trigger point' is the tension between the known, very ordinary, situation and the kingdom newness, upsetting in its very originality. Take the good Samaritan. There is an ordinary situation in terms of the times. A traveller is beaten, bruised and robbed. There is the extraordinary situation that a stranger—or rather, a member of a despised cut-away section of the Jewish family—comes along and does far more for the unfortunate traveller than the normal demands of a common humanity. This is the 'trigger point' where the listener is challenged to think again about who is the neighbour, what are the demands of effective love and from where can love be expected. Whether or not the words 'go and do in like manner' are Jesus' own words is not the important point. The parable itself pushes every open-minded listener to revise his or her attitudes and actions in regard to neighbourly love.

Each parable of Jesus calls for radical conversion. The parable remains suspended until a decision is made. Like every good pedagogy it calls for personal involvement and corresponding action. Even today the parables of Jesus make us think about life—our life—in face of the kingdom of God. Thus the parables of Jesus remain open-ended. They do not offer a neat definitive solution valid for all time. Even the sharp reorientation brought about by listening to the parables of Jesus does not allow for a static rest in new insights and action. If effective love is the point of a parable, the challenge of such love presents itself anew in each life situation. If the disclosure of God's kingdom strikes home in one situation, it will strike home anew in a different context. The parables do not allow us to settle in one comfortable view of

God, of self, of others. Rather they are an ongoing principle of auto-critique. 'Go and do in like manner' is an injunction which accompanies us all our days.

Justice before Stability

The death of Jesus

> 'For us the death of Jesus is, after all, a question
> put to God—to the God whom Jesus proclaimed.'[1]

THE death of Jesus was not an accident. Calvary was neither
an elaborate drama nor a tragic coincidence. It was certainly
not a historical irrevelance as Rudolf Bultmann at one time
argued. Jesus' identification with the sufferer and his criticism
of the wrongs inflicted in the name of God brought him to the
cross. His death was the outcome of his life project. There is 'a
more or less straight line from Jesus' eschatological message of
the Kingdom to the mystery of his Passion'.[2]

Jesus died for the same reasons that prophets die in every
age. He identified and spoke about the gap between how things
stood and how they should be. His openness to the suffering
round him impelled his protest against everything that took
from people's dignity. In calling people to justice, to love, to
responsibility and to freedom, he kept radical vision and keen
realism in tandem. Jesus the prophet was—and remains—the
great example of a believer without a loss of reality sense. His
experience of God as Abba grounded his vision of the future.

In announcing the kingdom, Jesus spoke for God. His life
and work are all in the name of the Father. His kingdom
preaching was an announcement of how God would have
things be. Thereby it was also a protest against the shabby
status quo. Where God willed *shalom, shalom* was in fact
denied. The rule of God permits no yoke, no thong of oppression. And yet, oppression was rife. Jesus castigated such
oppression with particular vehemence when it was practised by
those who claimed to speak for God. Quite accurately, the

'rulers in Israel' discerned the subversive thrust of Jesus' practice. They saw that he was questioning dominative power—*their* power—over others. The power of the law, which Jesus did not contest, had been arrogated to purposes for which it was never intended. Jesus protested at the sequestration of Israel's heritage by Scribes, Pharisees and others. These classes would prevent the small and the humble from access to their Father. The preaching of kingdom values was a dangerous challenge to encrusted patterns having little to do with justice, compassion, trust and simplicity. It was also a threat to those dominant groups which had battened on the weak through the abuse of socio-religious power.

The challenge posed by Jesus was disturbingly simple. It was a stern denunciation of present hypocrisy and blindness: 'You know how to interpret the appearance of the earth and sky, but why do you not know how to interpret the present time?' 'You tithe mint and dill and cumin, but you neglect to obey the really important teachings of the Law, such as justice and mercy and honesty.'[3] The challenge was also positive. It afforded glimpses of alternative ways of access to God through acts of solidarity with the victims of oppression as well as through table fellowship and acts of healing. These were symbolic or sacramental in being at once realisation of God's salvation and a pointer to something yet to come. Jesus met every request for healing even when the legal prescriptions did not so permit. Deliberately he placed human need above Sabbath prescription. In his dealings with women, with publicans, with despised and excluded classes of people, he showed the new and better way. What stronger example of this praxis than Jesus' espousal of the cause of the woman taken in adultery?

In human terms Jesus' death was his elimination by the order which he had put in question.[4] He had incurred the enmity of three powerful groups. He was hated by the courtiers of Herod for his fearless contempt of this weak but vicious ruler. Again, the Pharisees and the doctors of the law were severely criticised by Jesus for their formalism and rigour in application of the Torah (law). And in the volatile political situation presided over by Pilate, mention of a kingdom of God could provide a hostage to fortune. The Roman procurator had—and did use—the power to crucify those who threatened Rome's hegemony by political resistance. In the case of Jesus there is the macabre coincidence of these three sources of lethal repression—Herod, the Sanhedrin and Pilate—in securing his death.

There is every reason to hold that Jesus knew in advance the outlines of his approaching death. Although Matthew 23:37 may be the fruit of post-Resurrection faith it bears the memory of Jesus' reference to his death: 'Jerusalem, Jerusalem you kill the prophets and stone the messengers God has sent you.' Even while he was yet in Galilee the danger was becoming clear. Mark traces the descending curve of Jesus' success in preaching the kingdom of God. He seems to have been rejected in several cities—Bethsaida, Capernaum and Chorazain. According to Mark, Jesus' healing practice on Sabbath occasions and his defence of such healing brought about the conspiracy of Pharisees and Herodians to destroy him. It is a bitter irony that despite Jesus' preaching of the humanity of God, despite his opposition to repressive legalism, despite his preaching of good news to the poor, he was rejected even by his own, even in Nazareth. And the meaning of this for his own life would not have escaped Jesus. The total misunderstanding of his work subsequent upon the feeding of five thousand families marks the breaking point—from that point on Jesus withdraws from the Galilean ministry thence to set out for Jerusalem.

The gospels provide valuable clues to the significance of this pilgrimage. Some biblical scholars set it in the context of an Exodus. It is certainly a movement from rejection and misunderstanding in Galilee to danger and final elimination at Jerusalem. At all points, Jesus' practice incurs danger from those who are disturbed by his introduction of hope and vision to people whom they wished to keep under their own rule. Already, there is a menacing overtone to the arrival in Galilee of 'the doctors of the law who had come down from Jerusalem'.[5] It is by no means over imaginative to see Jesus going up to Jerusalem as a pilgrimage, a going-out-in-faith to a place where he would be in considerable danger. Only an unwarranted disinterest in the Jesus of history would claim that Jesus was unaware of his peril. His arrival at Jerusalem compounded the danger. One can but agree with Edward Schillebeeckx that 'from a particular moment in his career Jesus must have come to terms with the possibility, in the longer term probability and in the end actual certainty of a fatal outcome'.[6]

The stated grounds for Jesus' condemnation are not easily placed in a coherent whole. The passion narratives mention several charges raised at the Sanhedrin meeting. These charges sought Jesus' condemnation as a false prophet and a blasphemer. Mentioned too were an alleged threat to destroy the temple as well as the charge that Jesus had set himself up as Messiah. Jesus had consistently avoided the title Messiah—the only conceivable ground of the charge could be his triumphant entry into Jerusalem shortly before the Passover. From the view-point of the prosecuting authorities Jesus perhaps could be seen as a 'false prophet' and a 'blasphemer'. The measure of the false prophet was set by the Torah. At Deuteronomy 17:12 it was written: 'Anyone who dares to disobey either the judge or the priest on duty is to be put to death'. The presumption of Jesus was that although he held no office or authority from the Law, he had spoken for God in a startlingly new way. He had widened God's concern far beyond the confines of the law. The law of Israel did indeed articulate a hope in the coming salvation of Yahweh. However, this salvation had become limited to those who fulfilled the *minutiae* of legal prescription. It had come to exclude people deemed accursed and outcast. Jesus contested the exclusion.

He presumed to outstrip the traditions of the Rabbis in proclaiming God's graciousness to all. Whereas, the best of Israel's prophetic tradition had spoken of God's kingdom for the righteous and God's judgment for the unrighteous, Jesus extended the kingdom to the unrighteous.[7] This was indeed a provocation compounded by the outsider status of the carpenter's son from Nazareth.

The silence of Jesus before his accusers is a notable feature of his trial. He refused either to disown or even to justify his service of the kingdom of God. The silence was a critique whereby he placed his work above the judgment of any human tribunal. It may well have afforded a pretext for the unanimity of the Sanhedrin in deciding to hand Jesus over to the Roman authorities. Edward Schillebeeckx can write: '*contemptus auctoritatis*, holding Israel's highest authority in contempt, seems to me to be the Jewish legal ground for Jesus' condemnation'.[8] The guilt of the Sanhedrin was not in any breach of due process. Despite its hostility to Jesus it did not in fact condemn him to death. Its fault was to collude with the civil power in the maltreatment of one whose challenge was too disturbing to contemplate.

Jesus was put to death by the occupying power. There is a strongly political overtone to the title placed over the cross of Jesus: Jesus of Nazareth King of the Jews. According to Oscar Cullmann, 'Jesus was condemned by Pilot as a Zealot.'[9] In some respects, Jesus' preaching of the kingdom *was* sufficiently close to Zealotry to place him in danger from the Roman power once he entered Jerusalem. One cannot discern with any certitude how much of a threat Jesus posed in Roman eyes. Luke hints that Pilate wished to release Jesus. Yet Luke is favourable to Rome and may not be reliable on this point. At any rate there are sufficient overtones to Jesus' condemnation to discredit every view of his death as either non-political or a simple misunderstanding. Jesus was 'caught between the millstones of power'.[10] Religious establishment colludes with political establishment to eliminate one who was a threat to them both. The issue which led to his undoing was his concept and practice of the kingdom of God.

Jesus went to his death not eagerly but voluntarily. There is considerable evidence that he not only foresaw his death but also viewed it as the culmination of his witness to the kingdom of God. It is in this light one should interpret the references to his death as a 'ransom for many' and to his own placing the last supper in the context of the coming kingdom. At the same time we should not evade the tragic circumstances of the crucifixion. This death was marked by many signs of failure. Jesus died with a loud cry. The taunt 'He trusted in God' was not rebutted by any divine intervention. No matter how we interpret the words ascribed to Jesus—my God my God why hast thou forsaken me—one has to admit that Calvary leaves a question mark over Jesus' ministry to the kingdom. The question is not about Jesus' solidarity with the despised and the outcast. That solidarity stands as an enduring witness to

76

the greatness of Jesus of Nazareth. The question rather is whether such solidarity is forever doomed to failure. Is Jesus' life-stance doomed to be crushed by the malevolence of oppression? Is his good news for the poor set at nought by the silence of God? As a first step one must admit that Calvary poses a question about the silence of God in the very place where God's name is most lovingly invoked. The opening line of Psalm 53 ('My God my God why hast thou forsaken me') can indeed be interpreted as Jesus' dying prayer. Yet, it can also be taken as a cry of loneliness and abandonment. Its disturbing question cannot easily be ignored. Since Jesus had staked so much upon his father, since his life work stood for a specific message of God, his death is a God-question. Is God the God of Jesus of Nazareth? Or is God the God of all the forces which eliminated him?

The Scandal of Jesus' Death

The arrest of Jesus was followed by a debacle among his followers. With the possible exception of John, all the office holders of the post-Easter Church scattered and ran. It is true that there are shadings in the gospel accounts of this failure. Yet their common feature is the breakdown and dispersal of the disciples: 'They had thought that they had found in him the king who could never more be overthrown, and had become unaware the companions of an executed criminal.'[11] Constancy was shown only by the women (amongst them the mother of Jesus) most of whom had followed him from Galilee. Everyone with a vested interest faltered in courage and faith. The wry comment of the Emmaus narrative sums it well—'we had hoped...'.[12] As if to say: all theological hopes were shattered in the scandalous failure of the cross. This scandal lay heavily on the bright hopes raised by Jesus' words and actions. Perhaps he was mistaken? Perhaps his challenge in the name of God's kingdom was a presumptuous dream? Perhaps it was just another lesson that it does not pay to confront the great ones of this world even in the name of God? Notice that the gospels do not raise our modern problem of God. The questions raised there are about Jesus' work rather than about God. Is Jesus *the* prophet or just another dreamer? The question we can discern in the texts in the aftermath of the passion do not protest against God. They are rather evidences of an attempt to come to grips with the devastation wrought on people's hopes by the passion and death of Jesus. And it is from within a faith in the living God preached and witnessed by Jesus that the elements for an answer to the scandal of the Cross come.

In the writing known to scholars as Luke-Acts, the death of Jesus and his resurrection are placed in a contrast scheme. This scheme is expressed as follows: 'You killed him but God raised him up.' The contrast expressed an answer by converts to the taunt that Jesus was a false prophet. To this taunt they responded that Jesus had suffered the martyrdom reserved for true prophets. As evidence for this they cite his resurrection: God raised him up.[13] The tradition was extant in certain Jewish circles that the lot of the prophet was to be stoned. The contrast scheme places Jesus as a true prophet whose death is the outcome of his prophecy and whose exaltation is the seal of God on his life and work. It should be noticed that in this scheme of understanding, the death of Jesus is not singled out for its own sake. It is simply the outcome of Jesus' life-work, the end-point of the path he had trodden.

There is a second strand of tradition wherein Jesus' death is placed within the range of God's plan of salvation. Jesus' death is part of salvation history. It is an essential step in the working out of God's saving activity. The clearest expression of this tradition is at Mark 10:33-4—'the son of man will be handed over . . . they will condemn him . . . and kill him, but three days later he will rise to life.' This 'will be' arises from a long-standing Jewish conviction that the 'righteous one' inevitably suffers precisely as righteous. His suffering finds remedy only in God. The one who suffers most profoundly is the one who is most highly exalted by God (Ps. 18:18-20). The tradition attested to by Mark tries to place the death of Jesus in a comprehensible framework. Whereas crucifixion was anathema, Jesus could not be accursed. His is the suffering of the righteous one who therein is exalted. And so, it is argued, terrible suffering must precede the raising to glory—'the son of man must suffer many things and so enter into glory'.

Finally, there are clusters of tradition where Jesus' death is for others: 'He died for our sins and was raised for our justification' (Rom. 4:25). This interpretation of Jesus' death although widespread through the New Testament represents a late development.[14] Upon what does this insight into Jesus' death rest? Some exegetes suggest that we have here an application of the 'suffering servant' theology of Isaiah 53. Others look to late Jewish belief in the efficacy of a martyr's death as atonement for others. Both views have much to recommend them. Neither is absolutely cogent.

The Resurrection of Jesus

This is the hinge upon which the New Testament turns. The Exaltation-Resurrection suffuses everything that is said about Jesus. It is also an essential ingredient of the New Testament's understanding of God. The Exaltation-Resurrection of Jesus is an act of God. The subject of this action is God. It is God's answer to Jesus' life and death. It is the resolution of the paradox of the cross. There, the only silent voice was the voice of God. With the exaltation of Jesus the effective presence rather than the absence of God is attested.

The New Testament attests a clear message. Jesus of Nazareth is the one who has been raised up by the power of God. This is the Easter message expressed in brief, clear formulation—'Christ died for our sins and was buried, he rose on the third day according to the scriptures and appeared . . . '.[15] At Romans 10:9 we find the splendid formula—'If you confess that Jesus is Lord and believe that God raised him from the dead, you will be saved.' Paul makes it very clear that the Jesus who died and was buried is the one who was raised by the power of God. The one who died for our sins was raised for our justification (Rom. 4:25). The texts alluded to above contain a developed theology, viz. that Jesus is Lord and in appearing to Peter has entrusted a mission or commission. Whereas the preaching of Jesus pointed directly to his Father, this *kerygma* has as object both Jesus as Lord and his Father as the one who raised him from the dead.

There is an essential unity between the cross and resurrection. If there is no resurrection then the cross is essentially different from what we believe it to be. The cross prevents the resurrection from being a merely optimistic preaching separate from human suffering, disappointment and failure. That being said, everything the New Testament says about the ministry and death of Jesus is coloured by faith in his exaltation. Everything leads to Easter and all that Easter implies. And so, if we look to the God of Jesus Christ we must look at the resurrection proclamation of the New Testament. There is an order here. In the first place, there is an exaltation-resurrection *kerygma*. One finds this in brief clear formulas such as Galatians 4:4; Philippians 2:6; Romans 4:25; Luke 24:34. The subject of the action is God the Father. It is the Father who raised Jesus up and gave him a name which is above all names (Phil. 2:6). Jesus of Nazareth is the object or beneficiary of God's action—he was raised up on the third day (1 Cor. 15:3-5). The primacy of God's action is always in the forefront. The resurrection is an act of God. It is an initiative in favour of Jesus. Notice that the continuity between the one who died and the one who was raised is constantly stressed. The Easter preaching is rooted in the death of Jesus where God seemed silent: it proclaims the raising of the same Jesus as the breaking of that crippling silence.

Behind the kerygma lies an experience which motivates the proclamation that Jesus is risen. The Easter stories attest the experience whether as appearance accounts or as empty tomb narrative. One cannot reopen the long debates about the nature of the appearances and the status of the empty tomb tradition. But one can say that they bring us to the base of the conviction held by the followers of Jesus that the last word had not been said on Calvary. The scandal of the cross for the followers of Jesus was dissipated by another experience. Far from being a subjective re-assessment of Jesus, *this* experience attests the action of God in Jesus Christ. The act of God was the opposite of neglect or disavowal of Jesus. Rather it affirmed the meaning of his death. It also opened up a new understanding of God's intent in regard to Christ and to the world.

Here it is finally and unsurpassably revealed who God is: 'he whose power embraces life and death, existence and non-existence, who is creative love and faithfulness, the power of the new life, on which there is complete reliance even in the collapse of all human potentialities'.[16] It is, therefore, important to keep together Good Friday and Easter Sunday. Failure to do so cuts the bond between suffering and death in the cause of justice, on the one hand, and God's saving involvement with suffering humanity, on the other. The exaltation of the crucified Jesus is much more than the miraculous raising up of a dead man. It is an approbation of Jesus' preaching and practice. Here was more than a deluded enthusiast. God's seal is placed upon Jesus' presentation of God's kingdom, upon his claim that God was indeed a loving Abba. For those who had followed Jesus all was changed. The teaching, the healing, the life of devoted service lived by Jesus was seen to receive divine approval. Even more, in the resurrection Jesus was seen to be closely associated with the Father. Henceforth, all speech about God becomes pure idealism if it is divorced from the history of Jesus' life and death. On the cross the word and work of Jesus were shown to be one with his person. In the resurrection the person, word and work of Jesus were shown to be authenticated by the Father in whom Jesus placed his trust. One must then newly ask—as the earliest Christians asked—what has the life and death of Jesus to tell us about God?

In the first place, we are precluded from confining God to purely aesthetic or beautiful experiences. The ministry of Jesus was shocking rather than aesthetic. The 'pale Galilean' is a fiction of the imagination. There was nothing merely beautiful about Calvary. It was the tortured outcome of solidarity with the outcast and the despised. Only in the light of the resurrection can we say that God is wherever crosses are raised. If the resurrection and the cross are taken together, then the tormented question of whether the murderer is forever to have his foot on the neck of the victim is answered by a resounding No!

Here, then, is no mere drama. A cosmic history is unfolded before our eyes. It is a summation of the age-old conflict of injustice with justice, of loveless oppression with suffering love. The light Easter day sheds on Calvary is a startling, new thing. The New Testament reaches for many models to express this new thing—the reconciliation of a broken world (Col. 1:20), the justification or making-right of human beings before God (Rom. 4:25), the sealing of the hope of eternal life (1 Cor. 15), the expiation of sins through sacrifice (Hebrews). The dominant, although not exclusive, stress is on the initiative of God the Father: God was in Christ reconciling the world unto himself (2 Cor. 5:19). In the light of Easter, the cruelty and absurdity of crucifixion is not bypassed but rather is transcended. We have to do not with the unconcern or apathy of God but rather with the humanity and love of God.

And so one can speak about 'the crucified God'. This expresses God's involvement with Christ on the cross. For us the cross is the puzzling silence of God. In the light of Easter, it becomes the place where God is seen to be most deeply and painfully involved with humanity in Jesus who dared to call God, Father. If we take seriously the question posed by the cross of Jesus and the answer contained in his resurrection we can understand anew both the power and the love of God. God's love is powerful. God's power is love. And the cross is the place where both come together. Here in the light of Jesus' resurrection, God's loving power and powerful love can be discerned. It is precisely in the self-giving unto death that these are operative.

The God of Jesus Christ

With the pilgrim God in focus one can be permitted here to leave to one side some major concerns of systematic theology. The christological questions about the divinity of Jesus (which is taken for granted), the emergent ecclesiology of the New Testament, even the growth there of trinitarian theology, these are left aside. They have much to tell us about the God of Jesus Christ. Here, however, our search for the God of humaneness and of justice attempts to retrieve certain insights into the attitudes of God disclosed in Jesus. If we can say that the history of Jesus was attended at all points by his Father we can say that 'the face of the crucified (and risen) Christ is nothing less than the face of God'.[17] Even more, we can say with Albert Camus that in the night of Golgotha, in its very darkness, 'the Godhead... endures to the end the anguish of death including the depths of despair'.[18] This God is not the distant, unmoved God of theism. This God is certainly not the God who is appeased by human suffering and before whom people must abase themselves in order to be justified. In contrast to traditional theism we can say that God's very being is implicated in the cross of Christ—not inflicting or demanding its pain, but rather in solidarity with Jesus of Nazareth.

82

Have we the courage to say with Ernst Bloch that 'no God remains on high since none... is or ever was there'?[19] If the true God is implicated on Calvary in solidarity with the suffering Christ, we can leave behind forever the idea that God sits high in heaven abstracted from the fate of human beings. Calvary to Easter Sunday represents the destruction of that particular idol. The life and death of Jesus show forth that God is present even in the midst of weakness and agony. God cares enough about the woes of humankind to assume them, to suffer them, and even to die for them. There is no question of God's suffering due to deficiency or impotence. Yet it can be said that God assumes the history of sin and suffering in such a way that the very being of God is invested here. We cannot skirt around the staggering fact—a scandal to the Jew and a stumbling block to the Gentile—that God can become involved in suffering, pain and death. If God was in Christ 'reconciling the world to himself' this was first of all through solidarity with the suffering love of Jesus. Thereafter we may—indeed we must—see the presence of God wherever there is a sufferer or a victim. God is wherever crosses are raised. God is with the sufferer transfixed by pain or woe.

The Rending of the Temple Veil

In the gospel according to Mark the rending of the temple curtain signals the death of Jesus: 'the curtain hanging in the temple was torn in two from top to bottom'.[20] This curtain, thick and strong and solid, separated the Holy Place from the outer court. It reserved access to God for the priests and adult males. Thus, it excluded women and children, pagans and prostitutes, workers and peasants. It guarded the secret of the temple and claimed to signify the sacredness, the otherness, the reserve of God. The temple curtain represented a boundary between the sacred and the secular, the Jew and the Gentile, the men and the women. In excluding the prostitutes and others unclean, it bespoke a moralism at once harsh and narrow.

The Taiwanese theologian, Chaon-Seng Song reminds us that the sundering of the temple curtain was no half-hearted mediocre tear—'It did not tear apologetically and reluctantly...'[21] The death of Jesus, and the involvement of

83

God with Jesus on the Cross, spelled out the end of the divisions set up by the particularism of Jewish faith in its narrower interpretation. On the other hand, it marked the fulfilment of the promise recurrently formulated by Deutero-Isaiah of a kingdom for all people, a kingdom of justice, love and peace. Song is surely right to emphasise that 'from the Cross of Golgotha God moves to the "secular" oikumene'.[22] The old divisions were set at nought between the sacred and secular, between the narrow band of elect and the crowd denied access to God by mandarin classes of priests, Scribes and Pharisees. In this symbolic happening, Jesus' announcement of the kingdom to publicans and sinners is sealed. God is the God of all people, indeed of all creation. In the death and exaltation of Jesus the passion of God for all that God has made is seen in full strength and clarity.

The God of Jesus Christ is the God of all, just as Jesus himself was the man for all others. God is the God of all, not primarily in the sense that all paths lead equally to God. Without denying that there are indeed many paths by which people find God, one is here saying something else. It is that God in Jesus Christ seeks out all people and all places in salvific love. This is implied in Paul's unforgettable reminder that in Christ 'there is neither male nor female, neither Jew nor Gentile, neither slave nor free'.[23] In the ministry of Jesus, in his cross and resurrection, the full meaning of the temple of God (*templum Dei*) is made clear. God's dwelling with us is not in a temple made by hands. The mercy and loving kindness of God are indeed present. They are present in Christ's suffering and in the triumph and issue of that love on Easter Day. In this sense, 'The ruptured veil is the symbol of hope for those who have had to wait patiently and desperately in the outer court for such a long time for God's saving words for them.'[24]

'God first loved us'

A feature of the Exodus account is that God spoke first. Moses did not seek out God. He was addressed by God, called by God and sent by God. Thus the Old Testament account sees the great liberation of Exodus as the initiative of Yahweh. It is likewise with the New Testament. The narratives of Jesus' birth and infancy emphasise this: Jesus, the son of God, is conceived in the womb of the Virgin Mary by the power of the Holy Spirit. Paul, too, underlines the same priority in God's action. It is the Father of Jesus Christ who sent the son born of a woman, born under the law, that he might redeem those under the law (Gal. 4:4). Again, Paul speaks of the mystery of salvation hidden in the mind of God from eternity and now disclosed in the life, death and resurrection of Jesus. At one level the work of Jesus is particular and local. It is nothing more dramatic than three years in the life of a young teacher imbued with Hebrew wisdom and fired by an alternative vision. Yet New Testament reflection sees Jesus as the focus for a radically new departure. In Jesus, there is a new way of being human. Love of God and love of neighbour come together in an inimitable union in him. In him, humankind reaches out to and relates to God in a new way. Jesus' relation to his Father represents the high point of human development. Here humankind is at its best. Just as in Jesus is disclosed the nobility of humankind so also in him is shown forth the humility of God. In his life and death, the boundary between the divine and the human is crossed in our direction. God enters the human condition and becomes part of our human history. This is the prior movement of divine generosity. It is the truth of the text, 'God first loved us.' To cite the words of Pope Leo the great: God became man in order that man might become God.

There are several ways by which the approach of divine love finds expression in the New Testament. Paul develops the idea of reconciliation and recapitulation in Colossians and Ephesians. These are metaphysical concepts skilfully used by Paul to answer questions raised in his own day. To Pythagoreanism with its washing, its rites and its mysteries, Paul emphasises that indeed the whole world is reconciled to God by the cross of Jesus. This is a cosmic reconciliation. Things in heaven and things on earth are made one in the work of Jesus. The centre point of Paul's vision is Jesus who died on the cross. Yet the initiative is God's. Jesus is the image of the eternal God and the first-born of all creation. In him, God's fullness dwelled. One has to fight the dullness of routine hearing of this text to recover its staggering import—that Jesus of Nazareth should be the image of the eternal God. It is the text at Philippians 2:6 which best grapples with this:

> who, though he was in the form of God, did not count equality with God a thing to be grasped, but emptied himself, taking the form of a servant... and became obedient unto death, even death on the Cross.

In view of the divine self-emptying *(kenosis)* we can speak of the unselfish solicitude of God. Salvation is attained in the first place not by human effort but by divine solicitude. God spoke first and spoke in saving fashion. This tells us much about God. The God of Jesus Christ is not one who must be appeased. Much less is God the one who takes pleasure in pain and suffering. Rather, God approached us, entered our way and became embroiled in the conflict between good and evil. In the history of this just man, Jesus, that age-old conflict finds expression. The Christian affirmation is that he was not left alone in the conflict but was accompanied by his God and ours. The life and death of Jesus are the sacrament of the love of God in a sinful, torn world. That in Jesus 'God was reconciling the world unto himself' must surely push us away from the trivial images of a divine judge to the broader concept of the force of love who loves in eternity but also in time and even unto death.

The Withdrawal of Legitimation

Jesus died as an outsider, 'outside the camp'. He was neither priest nor rabbi: neither prince nor ruler. The very awfulness of his death placed him outside the polite circles of normality: 'Cursed be he who dies upon a tree.' Here is a critique of all establishments whether civil or ecclesiastical. Jesus lived as a poor man. He died as a subversive criminal. If God is fully involved in his life and death then, with Jesus, God has contested all power constructs as well as the 'wisdom' of the princes and hierarchs. In regard to such establishments, a 'hermeneutic of suspicion' rather than of legitimation is surely closer to the proper Christian stance. The hierarchs and the civil rulers colluded in the elimination of Jesus. It was they who hounded him to death. Why then is the option by God for the oppressed so often played down and even forgotten? At Exodus, God was on the side of the oppressed Hebrews, not of the allegedly divine Pharaoh. In Jesus, God was once again with the sufferer, this time on the cross. A most powerful element of subversion is thereby inserted in our history. The sufferer, not the inflicter of suffering, can expect that God is by his or her side.

We must not trivialise the terrible fate of the suffering, particularly the suffering of the weak. The memory of suffering will not allow an easy rest. The 'dangerous memory' of suffering should prevent us from settling with any *status quo*. It evokes a divine unease which is perhaps humankind's greatest compliment. If we can say that the God of Jesus was truly involved at Calvary then we can also say that God's solidarity with the sufferer is no mere aesthetic figment. The sad fact is that God has been used to legitimise oppression of every kind. As if the analogy between the rule of God and the squalid rule of tyrants could hold! The line, *regnavit a ligno Deus* (God ruled from a tree), breaks that assumption most effectively. If ever the name of God could be appropriated by the rich and the powerful, this cannot be done at the cross of Christ. One can only endorse the words of Rosemary Radford Reuther:

> It is this very idea of God as a great king, ruling nations as his servants that has been done away with by Jesus' death on the Cross. With Jesus' death, God, the heavenly Ruler, has left the heavens and has been poured out upon the earth with his blood. A new God is being born in our hearts to teach us to level the heavens and exalt the earth, and create a new world without masters and slaves, rulers and subjects.[25]

And yet the appropriation of God on the side of the powerful occurred in many of the nominally Christian centuries. God was made to underwrite the stability of empires, the depradations of colonialism, the harshness of law and order regimes. God was presumed to favour stability over justice, the ruler over the ruled. That presumption is not born out by the pattern of Jesus' life and death. Such presumption arises from the attempt to create God in our own image. The vengeful, judgmental God of law and order is the creation of vested interests rather than a true image of the father of Jesus Christ. Such a view of God must be judged at the bar of the cross-resurrection. There it is shown to be a deformation of the gospel rather than the fruit of it. In the light of the cross we can say that the God of the masters is not the God of Jesus Christ. In the phrase of liberation theology, the God of Jesus Christ is not the God of the slave owner, the colonist, the junta. These interests create their own God. They claim for their idols the name of the God of Jesus. In the light of Jesus' death and his Father's involvement in it, their creation is seen to be a sham and a fiction.

God's legitimation cannot be presumed by the mighty of this earth. The cross of Jesus should keep attention riveted where crosses are raised throughout this suffering world. Any theology which comforts the comfortable or afflicts the afflicted can hardly be other than alienating. A theology which is genuinely liberating must surely keep its eyes fixed on the cross of Jesus. Only from such a starting-point can any further speech about God (theology) be other than alienating. Perhaps this is intended by Edward Schillebeeckx's reminder: 'The word God can hardly be expressed otherwise than in a loud cry of indignation which at the same time expresses hope for reconciliation.'[26] It is not that legitimation is sought for *another* system in God's name—for that would simply be another attempt to harness God's freedom. The New Testament is very clear that it was the 'lords of this world' which crucified the Lord of Glory. What clearer indication can there be that the crucified Lord cannot be brought in on the side of those same princes and lords no matter what insignia they may wear.

The implication is surely clear. It is no part of faith in God to legitimate existing power constructs. In fact, the spirit of the gospel thrusts in the other direction. Jesus, Paul and James, each in his own way, relativise the pretentions of earthly powers. These powers exercise a quasi-divine claim which is nothing short of a deformation of the true God. When God is invoked to bless the militarism of great powers, as has happened in Great Britain and the US, or apartheid as in South Africa, one can suspect an abuse of the name of God. When the living God is used to lend respectability to patterns of domination, then an idol and not the true God is being invoked. The lesson of this is not to search around for a new conscription of God—as if to say, whereas once the divine right of kings held sway now we discern equally clearly the divine right of revolution. This would be a shoddy and dangerous bargain. No human programme can lay claim to divine sanction. If it does, it ends by becoming demonic. No programme, however just, can claim a monopoly of God's presence. Does this mean an eternally elusive God whose presence cannot be discerned anywhere? Does it entail a sceptical relativism whereby no distinction is made between justice and injustice, between human and inhuman political values? Does it mean a kind of night in which all swans are grey? By no means. We can indeed say that God is with those who struggle for the values enshrined in the paradigm that is Jesus' life and death. Above all, we can say that God is where suffering love attempts to confront the power of domination, exclusion, destruction and death. In a peculiar way these evil powers coalesce even when they have different points of departure.

Some Truths Revisited

I

The 'idea' of God: Is it healing or alienating?

Minimal acquaintance with comparative religion discloses a teeming diversity in people's idea of God. Gods, godlets and goddesses plentifully inhabit the pantheon of ages. Thus people have tried to gain some control of a threatening ambience, to glimpse meaning in life and to attain fragile security in the face of threat. Worship of gods/goddesses is not without self-interest. It evidences a need to propitiate the mysterious, to woo the manipulative arbiters of life's supports. Paul of Tarsus—by no means given to pathos—alludes to peoples' blurred recognition of clues to the divinity scattered here and there along their difficult path.[1]

Scholars have theorised on the birth of the 'idea' of God. It has been noted how much people's social context shapes that 'idea'. An agricultural people will worship the gods of fertility, of seasonal change, of growth and decay. A nomadic people will pay homage to gods of the road, mobile, unpredictable yet protective. The gods that people fashion almost inevitably reflect the prevailing social, economic and cultural interests. Noting this, many have argued that far from God making 'man' in the divine image, it is 'man' who has fashioned God after human likeness. There have been recurrent attempts to explain the idea of God by tracing the history of the idea. Such histories are normally fashioned with reductive intent. That is to say, they try to show that the affirmation of God is ill-judged and ill-founded. Thus, Sigmund Freud ties the idea of the Judaeo-Christian God to the relationship of the growing infant to its loved/hated father. God, in this explanation, is fashioned by the Oedipus complex. As we have seen, for Freud religion is an 'illusion'. The idea of God grows from the pathology of sexual immaturity. The step is short from this historical genesis to the claim that the affirmation of God is psychologically alienating and ontologically false.

Karl Marx charges that the idea of God is essentially alienating. He also attempts to disprove God through the supposed genesis of the idea. The idea of God, he claims, is an illusory projection of the unrealised hopes of the oppressed. The promises of religion are nothing other than palliatives for people ground down by economic and social oppression. Thus religion serves the dominant classes in an unjust society. Conveniently for them, it keeps the oppressed from outraged revolution. Behind this analysis—which carries more than a grain of truth—lies the argument of Ludwig Feuerbach. In his *Essence of Christianity* Feuerbach argues that God is merely the projection of human possibilities. All the good qualities to which humankind is heir by its very humanity are transferred to God. All the evil qualities which history discloses are attributed to humankind. Stated thus, it is a very bad bargain.

A contemporary theology cannot afford to ignore the Marxist critique. Statements of Christian teaching are not immune from group interest, partial insight and the will-to-power. Here, nonetheless, a different point is argued. The idea of God is not adequately explained by instances of its historical rise. The varied analyses of people's concept of God do not explain why the concept arises in generation after generation. Nor may the idea of God be discounted by a re-hash of its own pathology. Superstition, idolatry and alienation do not disprove the truth sought out in many forms of religious endeavour. There is a grain of truth in the theogonies of ancient societies. Just as myth cannot be reduced to fable neither can the tentative search for the divine be dismissed as utterly false. The search for the really-real poses a question which is not disqualified by the hypotheses of a Sigmund Freud or by the understandable strictures of a Karl Marx.

The 'Natural' Knowledge of God

Is there a 'natural' knowledge of God. Can people know God outside the explicit writ of the Christian gospel through their intelligence and reasonable good-will? Answers to this question have tended to diverge along confessional lines, with the Protestant tradition denying and the Catholic tradition affirming the possibility of a 'natural knowledge'. Martin Luther could say: 'reason is contrary to faith' and again '[reason is] prostitute of the devil'[2]. In the twentieth century Karl Barth spearheaded the refusal to consider even the possibility of a natural knowledge of God. Natural knowledge is a 'rank weed clinging even to what is apparently the soundest stalk, weakening it and finally killing it'.[3]

That God can be known by the light of reason rests on good scriptural authority, the book of Wisdom reminds us that:

> through the grandeur and beauty of the creatures we may, by analogy, contemplate the Author.

It asks:

> if they are capable of acquiring enough knowledge to be able to investigate the world, how have they been so slow to find its master?

And it answers:

> ... wretched are they ...
> who have given to things made by human hands the title of gods, gold and silver...
> likenesses of animals, or some useless stone, carved by some hand long ago.[4]

The Psalmists praise the creator on evidences discerned in nature both animate and inanimate. Yet, one should not claim too much here. There is no rounded natural theology in the Old Testament. However, the Old Testament has an extensive if largely implicit creation theology. It never denies the ability of the human spirit to know the creator, albeit at a distance. Paul is entirely consistent with the Old Testament wisdom in ascribing to people the ability to know God from creation: 'Ever since God created the world, his invisible qualities, both his eternal power and his divine nature have been clearly seen; they are perceived in the things that God has made.'[5]

In his sermon at Athens (Acts 17) Paul accepts that people of all times and places seek after God even if gropingly.[6] However, these texts show little optimism about people's success in arriving at a satisfactory knowledge of God from attention to creation. Wisdom 13 laments that instead of knowing God disclosed in creation, people confounded the artefact with the divine. Paul argues that 'instead of worshipping the living God [people] worship images made to look like mortal man or birds or animals or reptiles'. They become embroiled in idol-worship rather than serving their creator. Thus, 'they exchange the truth about God for a lie'.[7] Hence, Paul is led to extol the gospel as the privileged avenue of knowledge of God. For Paul the gospel is indeed God's power to save all who believe, both Jew and Gentile.

It would therefore be a mistake to see in these texts an *apologia* for speculation about God independent of the preaching of the God of Jesus Christ. Karl Barth's insistence is valuable—'it is on this ignorance of theirs in regard to God, which betrays itself even in their best possibilities but of which they are as such quite insensible, that Paul addresses these Athenians'.[8] And yet, there is an insistence within Catholicism although by no means confined to it, that God can be known by the human intelligence taking its point of departure in everyday experience. This insistence does *not* add up to a developed natural theology. It is a judgment of possibility rather than of fact. It does not canonise any particular form of natural theology. Nor does it specify either the manner or the route by which 'natural knowledge' of God is attained.

The First Vatican Council strongly reiterates the possibility of knowing God by the light of reason. The Council sets the question between two extremes. At one end is rationalism with its pretentions for the power of reason. At the other pole are fideism and traditionalism with their disqualification of every possibility of human reason knowing God except through tradition and blind obedience. Against the sacrifice of the intelligence demanded by fideism, Vatican I insists that God can be known with certitude by the natural light of reason from the things which God has made.[9] This claim presupposes that clues to the knowledge of God are all about us. Creation is a participation in the transcendent being of God. In some far-off way, every creature is a pointer to its creator. Vatican I presupposes that the human intelligence, made for the search for truth, can penetrate the surface of experience to glimpse a deeper, even divine, dimension. The lopsidedness and bias caused by sin cannot deprive us of that capacity. There is no pretention here to decide on how such knowledge is attained or on its content. Does it arise from 'an apprehension of contingency' given in the experience of growth, senescence and decay? Does it arise from the experience of obligation to a call higher than the pragmatic demand of human interests and human law? Do the experiences of beauty, of good, of truth point to something or someone beyond themselves. Any or all of these can be avenues to knowledge of God according to the tradition of the First Vatican Council.

III

The Desire for God

'I know you Lord when I feel all the desire and
the yearning that surpasses me,
the void of my discontent containing the broad
dimension of your immensity.'[10]

Augustine of Hippo speaks of a divine unease innate to us as human beings. Unforgettably he puts it, 'Thou hast made us for thyself O God and, our hearts cannot rest content until they rest in thee.' Again, Augustine speaks of a tendency or thrust (*pondus*) which, seeking in all directions, nonetheless has an ineradicable orientation towards God. Later on, the best of scholastic thought considered the natural desire to see God. Aquinas speaks of a natural desire to know the first cause of things. This desire can only be satisfied by the vision of God. St Thomas also adverts to the role of 'wonder' or intellectual enquiry. Enquiry thrusts to know the cause of every effect. Aquinas argues that such a desire cannot be illusory. All minds desire to know God. Since this is a natural desire it cannot be in vain.[11] In his realistic treatment of the human search for happiness St Thomas provides a systematic examination of appetition or desire. Just as our intelligence seeks the full horizon of truth, the will reaches out for universal good. Only a universal good can fill this quest.[12] Truth and good are at once the goal and the origin of all human action. It is the badge of humanity to seek to know truth and to seek out good. For St Thomas, and the medieval tradition, it is not merely the philosopher who seeks out wisdom and value. Nor is it simply the contemplative who comes to know God in his/her contemplation. Rather, each person exercises an implicit knowledge and love of God.[13]

Aquinas, then, is not the rigid metaphysician he is cast as being. In fact, he brings together the mystical and the rational dimensions of the intelligence in one movement. Whether one starts with the strictly rational type of consideration (as, for example, the five proofs) or with the more free-ranging devotional or mystical approach, one is carried by a natural dynamism (*pondus naturale*). This dynamic is common to philosopher, mystic and indeed to every man and every woman. The delimitation of the critical reason from the mystical search is perhaps too rigid. It may make sense on paper but it is not the stuff of life. On this point, Aquinas is on the side of the broader, freer movement, not of rigid delimitations.

Clearly this desire can run to seed. It can recreate idols, hypocrisies, self-serving interests. If it is not attended by moral restraint it *will* run to seed. Claims about the knowledge of God, therefore, must be controlled by the critical principle that God eludes every creation of our hearts and minds and wills. *Deus semper maior*, God is always greater than our ideas, our images, our desires. To rest in these is clear evidence of misunderstanding the mystery of God. Aquinas also wrote: 'If you think to have understood, then you have misunderstood God.' *Si comprehenderis non est Deus.* Again Augustine's never-ending search is exemplary even in our own day. Believing that the surest journey is the journey inwards, he searches for God by attending to the inner life. For Augustine the human soul is a privileged witness to God. Nevertheless, it can only take us so far. Thus, in the tenth book of the *Confessions* Augustine says:

> Now to thee I speak, O my soul, thou art my better part.
> For thou quickenest the mass of my body, giving it life,
> which nobody can give to a body.
> But thy God is even unto thee the Life of thy life.[14]

On the other hand, if with Paul and the Psalmists Augustine attends to the witness of nature as evidence of God he still will say:

> I asked the earth and it answered me 'I am not he'; and
> whatsoever are in it confessed the same. I asked the sea
> and the deeps, and the living creeping things and they
> answered, 'We are not thy God, seek above us.' I asked
> the moving air and the whole air answered, '... I am not
> God.' I asked the heavens, sun, moon, stars, 'Nor are we
> the God whom thou seekest.' And I replied unto all the
> things which encompass the door of my flesh: 'You have
> told me of my God, that you are not he; tell me something
> of him.' They cried out with a loud voice, 'He made us.'[15]

IV

The Proof of God's Existence

> 'There is and can be only one proof: in the whole ques-
> tionable nature of man seen as a totality.'[16]

In the anti-modernist reaction of the early twentieth century, maximal claims were made for the traditional proofs for the existence of God. Whereas the First Vatican Council was content to emphasise that God could be known from consideration of created evidences, the anti-modernist oath went further.[17] It enjoined the profession that 'the origin and goal of all things can be known with certitude and therefore even be demonstrated by the natural light of reason through the things that have been made, i.e. through the visible works of creation, as a cause is known through effects'. The new elements here are (a) demonstration (b) through visible effects (c) yielding a knowledge of God as 'a cause is known through effects'. Vatican I did not speak of demonstration, i.e. rigorous proof. Nor did it limit its purview to 'visible effects'. Thus it left the door open to a broader argument from 'experience'. Again it does not refer to an argument from causality as such. It would seem that one strand within Thomist theology, viz. neo-Thomism, was attempting to harness the Vatican decree to the proofs elaborated by themselves. There is a cost to this procedure. As the proofs come under question or are found wanting in clarity, the danger increases that the very affirmation of God will be dismissed as irrational or muddled. In any case, the deliberation of Vatican I should not be identified with the anti-modernist oath. The council's vindication of the role of reason is quite different from the tenets of a particular movement within scholastic theology.

How, then, does it fare with the 'proofs for the existence of God'? In regard to any one 'proof' there are many counter-objections. For every proof a counter argument can be produced. That is not to say that these proofs are fallacious. Yet, they have to be hedged in by so many qualifications that the average man or woman will feel that the matter remains as unclear as before. Have the learned proofs for the existence of God not become 'an ingenious cerebral thought-construct which ... for the average man remains abstract, opaque ... and without convincing force'?[18]

This is not the whole story. One cannot rest the affirmation of God on direct experience or on naked authority. No-one has ever *seen* God. Few can subscribe to André Frossard's hardy announcement: 'God exists, I have met him.'[19] This is a protestation rather than an argument. It can be matched by equally impassioned avowals of the absence of God. Appeals to authority or to loyalty derogate from the God-given autonomy of critical reason. It is true that Immanuel Kant wrote: 'I have found it necessary to deny knowledge, in order to make room for faith.'[20] Yet, Kant also felt it necessary to formulate practical reasons for affirming the existence of God even as he demolished the theoretical proof. Some form of justification for its reasonableness is required if faith in God is to be a human thing.

The disproofs of God's existence need critique as much as

97

do the traditional proofs. These, too, arise from a prejudice or prior option. The objections of Karl Marx and Ludwig Feuerbach are clearly ideological. In essence, they persist in arguing: God must die in order that man may live. One must persist in asking: is this so? Is not the problem the abuse of the name of God in order to serve vested interests? Many a contemporary believer will accept Marx's view of alienation but will claim that God need not be an alienating concept or reality. And so, while respecting Marx's protest, such a contemporary believer will insist upon the affirmation of God.

From the seventeenth to the nineteenth century attacks were made on the philosophical move from the contingent to the necessary, from the empirical to the metaphysical, from the phenomenal to the noumenal, from the apparent to the real. David Hume's radical demand for verification, Immanuel Kant's critique of theoretical reason, Ludwig Wittgenstein's criteria of meaning, all have thrown the balance against metaphysical statements. Here again, one must insist: this is not the whole story. These limitations must not be allowed to paralyse us. The empirical constriction has to be met head on. If it claims that we can never know more than we can touch then it is self-contradictory. It outstrips its own evidence and thereby contradicts itself. And so the point is repeated: even if the proofs of God are not universally cogent, neither are the disproofs.

There is yet another view long associated with the Protestant tradition but by no means exclusive to it. It disqualifies every proof as an idolatrous disrespect to the living God. It asks, 'Can God still be God in a proof?' Are we not reducing God to a physical or mathematical object? For Karl Barth, a proven God is an idol. It has nothing to do with the God of Jesus Christ. It is merely a plaything of human interests and prejudices.

It must be admitted that 'proofs' of God's existence—if such there be—are not like mathematical theorems. They lack the rigid self-consistency of mathematical operations. Perhaps St Anselm's ontological proof comes closest to these operations with its deduction of God's existence from its prior definition. Apart from this, the proofs are not to be cast in the mould of mathematical demonstration. They can pretend neither to the clarity nor to the self-consistency of mathematical discourse.

As has been pointed out by Anthony Flew, none of the proofs for the existence of God is capable of strict verification or falfisication. In terms of the principle of verification/falsification the proofs claim either too much or too little. They establish too much: for the extrapolation from the data of experience is regarded as fallacious. If the canons of David Hume are followed, traditional metaphysics is merely the logic of illusion. Its affirmation of a universal principle of casuality, in the post-Kantian view, no longer makes sense. The proofs establish too little: for the affirmation that God exists does not allow for any possibility of falsification. Nothing counts against it. Anthony Flew puts it well:

> Someone tells us that God loves us as a father loves his children. We are reassured. But then we see a child dying of inoperable cancer. His earthly father is driven frantic in his efforts to help, but his heavenly Father shows no obvious sign of concern. Some qualification is made—God's love is not a 'merely human love' or it is 'an inscrutable love'...we are reassured again. But then perhaps we ask: what is this assurance of God's (appropriately qualified) love worth, what is this apparent guarantee really a guarantee against?[21]

Undoubtedly, one is driven to a greater humility about the proofs for God's existence. As traditionally framed, they come increasingly under question. One might ask: do they convince only those who already accept the reality of God on other grounds? Perhaps so. One has also to say that the denial of God is as much a faith as is the affirmation of God. One might note Kant's avowal that the same grounds which disqualify the 'proofs' for God's existence also disqualify the assertion of the non-existence of God. Kant asks, 'From what source could we...derive the knowledge that there is no supreme being as the ultimate ground of all things?'[22] Are the alternatives either agnosticism or blind faith?

One can admit the limits of pure reason and yet insist upon the importance of critical understanding within faith. Failure to make this insistence cuts faith adrift from reason and relegates faith in God to an irrational sentiment or to blind obedience. One can concur with many of the objections to proofs of the existence of God while insisting that reason is not atheist, that atheism is not the (only) reasonable conclusion from the data of common human experience.[23] There is much to recommend John Macquarrie's suggestion that at the heart of every proof is an anthropological rather than a cosmological statement. The proof of God's existence attempts to articulate or explicate the experience of contingency.[24] It starts with an experience of oneself and of one's world and tries to draw out the full implications of that experience.

We cannot explain our existence. Rather we experience it as at once something given and yet endangered. In its very threatened character we perceive its gift. An experience of this kind never occurs in laboratory conditions. It is not clinical, detached or objective. It is self-involving, existential—in the most vital sense. When we experience our living, moving and having being, in its goodness and its fragility, we touch upon mystery—something affecting us deeply while yet eluding intellectual dissection or analysis. In experiencing our own contingency, our lack of control of our cherished existence—we have to do with an unknown-known, an untouched-touched. Edward Schillebeeckx rightly speaks of a direction of our conscious ignorance. In knowing that we do not fully know, in understanding that we do not fully understand, we are directed in a particular way. Aware of the limits of our being and our knowing, we can ask about something or someone who, transcending these limits, supports our being and our knowing. As we do so—if we do—we draw upon two poles of experience. One pole is our innate capacity to seek after an explanation commensurate to each question. The other is our objective situation which triggers the search for explanation or meaning.

If we accept this approach to the 'proofs' we will admit that they are not proofs as commonly understood in the sciences. They depend too much on the personal factor to qualify as scientific proofs. Yet, this need not cause us to lose nerve. After all, there are different kinds of evidence for different kinds of experiences. We will admit, with Barth and Tillich as well as with Newman, that God is not at the end of a neat syllogism. A purely theoretical or academic formulation turns to dust under our very pen or tongue. The 'proofs' start with an invitation to view oneself and others and world in a particular way. They then attempt what Hans Küng calls 'a clarifying illumination of the always problematical experience that invites man to a positive decision'.[25] This is not an appeal to blind faith or to authority. If 'proofs' are to stand they must make their arguments coherently and rigorously. Yet, they will also avoid any totalitarian argument or brow-beating.

The 'proofs' of God's existence, however they be framed, articulate a knowledge more original than words, concepts or even explicit logic. At their best, they explain how our knowing and our desiring (particularly when bent upon questions of meaning and value) bring us up against the mystery which touches us while always eluding us. Karl Rahner insists that each 'proof' of God's existence simply tries to articulate an experience deeper than any formal pattern of reasoning can fully express.

A 'proof' of God's existence is an attempt to show that we are always in touch with the mystery of our being 'in our intellectual and spiritual experience whether we reflect on it or not, whether we freely accept it or not'.[26] Any proof of God's existence must henceforth take the path of reflection on one's own experience as a being-in-the-world torn between rootedness and rootlessness, between security and anxiety, between the gift of and the threat to existence. As one comes up against the limits not simply of oneself but of all things human, as one touches upon a nameless 'other', the stances one takes are the result of free, unforced option. Here we cannot be pushed. We are left free. We *may* articulate the name of God. St Thomas was not correct when at the end of each of his five ways he said, 'and this all understand to be God'. Some indeed will name God; others will reserve judgment. Neither option is to be pilloried. Hence, the 'proof' of God's existence is not quasi-scientific. It is not an extension of cause and effect as postulated in physics or psychology. In a remarkable *allocutio* Pope John Paul II makes this clear:

> Scientific proofs in the modern sense of the word, are valid only for things that can be perceived by the senses,

because it is only on these that we can use the tools of research and verification that science makes use of ... To want a scientific proof of God would mean to bring God down to the level of the creatures of our world and thus to make a methodological mistake about what God is. Science must recognise its limits and its inability to reach the existence of God, something it can neither affirm nor deny.[27]

If we are speaking of proofs in the register of physics or mathematics then proofs of God's existence do not qualify as proofs. One can then say that scientific proofs of God are not possible. Scientific judgments cannot be made about God since God is not in space and time. However, to use a phrase of Hans Küng, there is an 'indemonstrable content' to the proofs which remains valid. Through this content we are put in the way of providing an answer to questions raised by, although not answerable by, scientific reflection.

For example, some of the most eminent physicists have underlined the apparently inexhaustible mystery of the physical universe. The eighteenth-century model of the world as a self-regulating mechanism has become obsolete. At the levels of the infinitely small and the infinitely great, hitherto unsuspected complexity has evoked the revolutionary language and concepts of the 'new physics'. Reflecting on this, Albert Einstein felt driven to speak of 'the rapturous amazement at the harmony of natural law, which reveals an intelligence of such superiority that, compared with it, all systematic thinking and acting of human beings is an utterly insignificant reflection'.[28]

In the *allocutio* cited earlier, Pope John Paul II referred to questions raised by science about 'an immensity, a harmony, a purpose that cannot be explained in terms of causality or by means of the resources of science alone...'.[29] Neither philosophy nor theology can provide us with new evidence for another kind of 'proof'. However, they can enable reflection upon the bases of coherence, intelligibility and rationality. Reflecting thus in dialogue with the new physics, both philosophy and theology can present us, whether we be Christian or not, whether we be scientist or not, with the choice of affirming a ground of life, of being, of intelligibility, of reality.

Again, the human sciences, psychology and sociology and history, can leave us with an unanswered question when they have brought us to their own limit. The question is about 'a profounder rationality and thus of something or someone capable of answering our inner needs, needs which the very progress of science makes more acute'.[30] Thus, the question is about existential rootedness, whether life is a blessed gift or an unmitigated blight, whether there is a goal fulfilling of all, whether our thinking and aspiring are oriented to a nothingness or to a fullness.[31] This is asked not just by religious people but by many others for whom religion has ceased to have either hold or attraction. Here too philosophers and theologians can have a word to say. Not peremptorily but in terms of elucidation of choice. Not as a knock-down argument against which there is no recourse.

Finally, there is the question of a moral or ethical order 'in which the dignity of man, of every human being, would be securely guarded and encouraged'.[32] This question is thrust upon us by experience of the absence of such an order. The prevailing order is, and always has been, one where the dignity of humankind is daily infringed by oppression and repression. It is an order where selfishness expels all possibility of brotherhood and sisterhood. An order in which the dignity of every human being would be guarded and encouraged remains a *utopia*. Aspired to constantly, it escapes our grasp with grim consistency. Do the aspiration and its fulfilment represent an absurd wish or do they rest on a personal, supra-individual base. One says 'personal' and 'supra-individual' since such an order, being about relations between persons, requires a foundation which is both personal and supra-individual.

Today those who present proofs for the existence of God show a certain humility. However, their tentativeness is not capitulation. The proofs are not valueless. Each kind of traditional proof—the cosmological, the teleological, the moral—has a certain validity. To cite Hans Küng again, each has an 'indemonstrable content' which retains its value despite relinquishment of any claim to be beyond dispute. Each sketches out some basic requirement if our world is to have an intelligibility deeper than the procedures of sicentific method can offer. Each contains a discipline and a rigour of thought lacking in both commonsense knowledge and the aphorisms of everyday wisdom. The proofs cannot define God into existence. That would be tantamount to blasphemy. Nor will they convince everyone. Perhaps they will convince no more than a small minority. Their most valuable contribution is to help some people to the threshold of something greater—the affirmation of the living God. That affirmation is not in the gift of either philosophy or theology. As for the proofs, they 'do not loose their validity...because they have lost their power to prove. They amount to a confirmation of faith by intellectual operations.'[33]

V

The Affirmation of God

A proof of God's existence is not the same as the affirmation of God. The proof must serve the affirmation. Otherwise, it is virtually useless. Again, one can accept the proof yet remain short of the affirmation. In the latter there is a personal investment which goes well beyond proof. When the proofs have raised the right questions and, indeed, stated good answers, there is still a further step which is not taken by theoretical reason alone. W. Pannenberg puts it well:

> The proofs of God...retain their significance as elaborations of the questionableness of finite being which drive man beyond the whole compass of finite reality. But they do not provide the answer to this question.[34]

The traditional proofs state an answer. Yet since the proposition 'God exists' is a costly self-involving proposition it is not identical with understanding a chain of reasoning. The affirmation 'God exists' is not like the proposition 'the earth is round'. For it is a taking up of a position on a matter of importance on one's life and death, one's hopes and prospects, one's duties, rights, and obligations.

There is a claim, by no means confined to Roman Catholic theology, that every human life implicitly affirms God. St

Thomas Aquinas argued this in regard both to our knowing and to our free choice. We affirm God implicitly in every act of judgment and in every choice of the good. *Deus implicite cogniscitur in quolibet cognito.*[35] This arises from Aquinas's view of truth and good as participations in the first truth (*veritas prima*) and ultimate good (*summum bonum*). However, it is also an anthropological statement about the reach of human knowing and willing. The depths of the person touch upon mystery and the presence to mystery enables us to embrace every partial truth and good precisely as truth and good.

The great exponents of this view are Henri de Lubac and Karl Rahner. Every instance of knowledge, every exercise of freedom is a transcendental experience. Each act of knowing or of free choice is based upon a pre-reflective experience of our intellect's grounding in absolute being and of our will's aspiration to absolute good. Rahner claims that our knowing is always 'a real if implicit knowledge of God'.[36] An approach of this kind bursts asunder any narrowing of the affirmation of God to propositions or dogmas. It does not deny or contradict these. Yet, it emphasises an experience in knowledge and freedom, a knowledge before a knowing, which is implicitly the affirmation of God. This experience is the root of every subsequent Yes or No in regard to God. Available to all people, it heads towards articulation as an affirmation of God. The explicit affirmation of God will vary in accordance with religious and cultural context. It will be more complex than a uniform intellectual formulation. Faith can never be identified with belief or creed. Underlying belief and creed there is, and must be, a religious conversion. Such conversion is about loyalty to truth and a readiness to *do* the truth. Again, the affirmation of God includes a readiness to be a pilgrim in service to the truth even when service demands that one enter paths hitherto uncharted. One can say that 'the ultimate religious fact does not lie in the realm of doctrine or even individual self-consciousness'.[37] These have their place which is indeed an important one. Nonetheless, they are void and empty if not shot through with faith, hope and love.

It is, therefore, a monstrous presumption to disqualify as either unavailing for salvation or idolatrous the many ways people have attempted to name God. The arrogant dismissal of every affirmation other than the one framed in explicitly Christian terms can no longer stand. Major documents of Vatican II recognise the value of other religious approaches. In particular, they recognise the primacy of conscience in framing an affirmation of God. This is neither a vagueness about truth nor indifference to it. It is not a twilight in which all colours merge. Rather, it is a recognition that religious truth is a pilgrim truth attained only by hard-won stages ever in fidelity to the light. If all affirmations of God arise from an unspoken experience of mystery, then one must allow for a broad range in people's concepts and judgments. The truth cannot be constricted to a nutshell or contained in a neat formula. Even in the apparently hostile contradiction of atheism one should first look for the affirmation contained in its very denial. Desmond Fennell's remark has considerable point: 'The denial of God's existence can be a desperate attempt to preserve sanity and to achieve some kind of intelligible basis for love.'[38]

St Thomas's distinction between our ways of expression and what we endeavour to express is of enduring value. There is always a surplus of the *things signified* over the *ways of signifying*. The distinction is appropriate to our attempt to understand and express the deeper things in life—love and hate, joy and sorrow, belief and unbelief. We can know more than we can express. To advert to this surplus is already a deepening of understanding. Informed ignorance brings us much further than pretentious claims to knowledge. Since we do not have a hotline to God it is better to live with a 'reverent agnosticism' (E. Gilson). Our choicest images, analogies, metaphors and parables, simply point into the mystery. They are coloured by our history, culture, prejudices and assumptions. They direct us on a particular path. We hope and believe it is the right path. However, they do not capture the reality. God's 'goodness' will always remain ahead of the profoundest human knowledge. That otherness is symbolised by the biblical 'hiddenness'. Yet, with the medieval tradition we say that despite our limitations God does not remain unknowable. Our faltering knowing and speaking can point beyond themselves to a barely glimpsed reality. St Thomas has gently reminded us that our cherished doctrines point beyond themselves to the ungraspable reality (*articula autem non terminant ad verba sed ad rem*).[39] There is an extraordinary richness to St Thomas's repeated insistence that the highest knowledge we can have of God is that God remains above all that we can ever know or grasp. Notice here the fine balance between knowing and unknowing. The knowledge is real. Yet it is aware of its limitations. It is an agnosticism, not of emptiness but of fullness.

For much of modern philosophy this approach is radically questionable. The school of linguistic analysis rejects even the meaningfulness of the affirmation of God. So too does the brusque pragmatism of both late capitalism and Leninism. For both, theological discourse is a subject without an object. For the anguished rejection inset to existentialism, the affirmation of God is a shot in the dark signifying nothing except a contradiction. We have already adverted to the linguistic analysts from A. J. Ayer to Anthony Flew and noted their claim that a statement is meaningless if it is neither self-evident nor empirically falsifiable/verifiable. On these grounds, the affirmation of God is judged to be either an idiosyncratically private view of reality or part of a language game. At most, it is a curious shorthand for an ethical programme of life. If it is to have any meaning, it requires thorough-going reformulation. It means a demythologising which discloses much about the affirmer and nothing about God.

For philosophical as well as for theological reasons, one must contest this constriction to the narrow range of empirical verification-falsification. It is the outgrowth of a belief that the really-real is only what can be measured. This is a pragmatic reduction. The reduction has been questioned by thinkers as diverse as G. Marcel and H. Marcuse. It is a matter of experience that human faith, cherished hope and personal love run well beyond what can be measured. To say this is far from discounting critical reason. It is rather to resist the imperialism of pure reason as conceived of by the Enlightenment, and of practical reason as framed in *bourgeois* ideology.

Since the affirmation of God involves the whole person, mind and heart and feeling, it is indeed a personal stance in regard to the really-real. It is not reducible to one field of knowledge amongst others. At its best it pervades all the dimensions of our existence. It is not sectoral like the disciplines of science or mathematics. As we have argued, it is rooted in an apprehension of that most intimate relation between God and man/woman, between creator and creature. Thus, it is unique. It is as unique as the act of love. As no two people experience life in exactly the same way, neither can two people be said to affirm God in identical fashion.

Notwithstanding the personal quality of the affirmation of God there is also a communal or public side to belief in God and its expression. In so far as people know God, they do so within a tradition. Granted the priority of a person's conscience in affirming the living God, one must advert to the mediation of symbols, creeds and witness afforded by a tradition. It would be a distortion of the Christian tradition to underplay its reality claim about God. Despite the shading between the symbolically-real and the empirically-real endemic to all theological language, there is nevertheless a claim to touch upon reality. Theological language is not purely symbolic or simply metaphorical. James P. Mackey argues, 'People cannot encounter a power in this world and name it God without thereby forming some image or concept of what divinity is like "in itself".'[40] However, we cannot capture or programme, much less predict God. The claim that God *is* or is such and such remains irredeemably analogical. Understood aright, it leaves room for mystery at all points. And yet, since it rests upon disclosure-situations (glimpses of a blessed or sacred present) it acknowledges an elusive yet real presence. It attempts to speak about the real rather than the unreal, about the substance rather than the shadow. At this point we have to do with confession as distinct from simple affirmation. Or rather, all along we have been speaking about confession in the sense of giving thanks, worship and praise.

The Danger of Distortion

The Marxist protest underlines the possibility of ideological perversion of speech about God. For many people the great obstacle to faith in God is not intellectual argument. It is fear of alienation—that there is a conflict between faith in God and human flourishing. For humankind to be fully human, God must go. E. Bloch argues 'where the great world-ruler holds sway, there is no room for freedom, not even the freedom of the children of God nor of the mystical-democratic figure of the kingdom...'[41] From another angle, the critique of ideology articulated by Jurgen Habermas adverts to the interests served through the manipulation of knowledge. Even the most hallowed doctrines of Christianity (or of any other religion) can skew reality in favour of vested interests.[42] More than once, God has been 'used' as an ideological counter within and without the Churches. Politicians, officials and mandarins of all kinds have tried to harness God's name to their own schemes and programmes. More often than not this abuse has come from the right wing of the political field. The living God is then made into a legitimation mechanism for causes and projects which have nothing to do with the will of God. The shell of theological affirmation remains, but now the false God of money, power, law and order, racism and statism is worshipped. This can happen in rituals and professions which are nominally Christian.

Edward Schillebeeckx has rightly complained of the 'ayatolahization' of politics. This is totally different from the political implications of faith in God. It is nothing more than the abuse of the name of God to serve partial and selfish ends. The abuse must be clearly identified as such. It leads to the destruction of people and the dishonouring of the name of God. From South Africa to Ireland, from Iran to the United States, from Argentina to Great Britain, people reach for the name of God to legitimise the illegitimate, to justify the unjustifiable. When apartheid is legitimated from the Bible or national security is justified as defence of Christian order, then God is being abused. The outstanding witness on this in our century is the Barmen Declaration (1934).[43]

The affirmation of God is not a certitude which, once acquired, can be tucked away in the recesses of the mind. There is a moral dimension to it, an element of choice, commitment and self-involvement. As with any other such commitment it requires renewal and reinforcement. It is always liable to decay unless rejuvenated by integration into one's overall life pattern. Weary disillusion, the wintry experience of God, can lead one to doubt or deny what one has affirmed in better times. The heart grows weary, the emotions become bleak.

People can be led to drop their explicit affirmation of God. A growth in critical awareness does not necessarily mean the denial of God or suspension of belief. Yet, it demands a corresponding effort to keep alive what otherwise might wither through premature suspicion, narrowness of vision or simple conformism. Henri de Lubac remarks that 'whenever it abandons a system of thought, humanity imagines it has lost God'.[44] For this very reason, the affirmation of God needs renewal not simply at the level of mind but also in the heart and will. With Hans Küng one can say:

> [Belief in God is] not grasped once and for all, but constantly to be freshly realised: belief in God is not secured against atheism unassailably and immune from crisis by rational arguments. Belief in God is continually threatened and—under pressure of doubt—must constantly be realized, upheld, lived, regained in a new decision: even in regard to God himself man remains in insoluble conflict between trust and mistrust, belief and unbelief. But, throughout all doubts and precisely in this way, the affirmation of God is proved in fidelity to the decision once made: it becomes a tried and tested belief in God.[45]

The God of Life, Gladness, Daring

I

'The Glory of God is Humankind fully alive'
Irenaeus of Lyons

LIKE all tradition, the tradition of belief in God is two-headed. It is both gift and threat. It can bring liberation and alienation. It has nourished hope, love and collaboration. It has motivated selflessness, mercy and justice. Unfortunately, it has also spawned war, legitimated injustice, and fomented division. We cannot, we must not, remain heedless of the blind spots in the theist tradition. However, if we stand within the tradition of explicit faith in God we cannot, we must not, neglect the retrieval and the re-integration prerequisite for the survival of all tradition. Bishop David Jenkins's question has a salutary impact. Is our God worth believing in? Is our God too small? Arbitrary? Uncaring? Punishing the small man's peccadillo while remaining unresponsive to Auschwitz, Hiroshima and the Gulag Archipelago? Is not the God intolerable who finds car keys but who is absent from the repeated holocausts through the generations. How dare we affirm God in trivialities and fail to be troubled by people's tragedies? Jenkins's particle *our*—*our* God—is important to note. *Our* God is not always the God of Jesus Christ. We make God out to be capricious, guilt inducing and cruel. Our insecurity and lack of love create a God closer to George Orwell's Big Brother than to the gracious Father of Jesus Christ.

Meister Eckhart spoke of that 'last and highest parting when for God's sake [one] takes leave of God'. One does *not* leave

God behind. One moves beyond one's images of God. Repeatedly. Endlessly. One has to seek out less inadequate masks for a God who must wear some mask in order to come within our ken. When Christians say to their Churches: 'That I can't believe'—they are not necessarily reneging on the faith. They may simply be pointing out that God is greater than everything the Churches have allowed God to be. When atheist or agnostic enters a protest, whether quiet or stridently hostile, he/she challenges the tradition of faith to examine itself in its witness to the living God. Yet it was within the Church that the memory of Christ was nourished and understood as a disclosure of God. There it was insisted that God is greater than all our imagining: *Deus semper maior.* Thus the pressure was maintained to remain on pilgrimage. We lapse into idolatry if we allow the comfort of stability to detain the search for God. However, thanks to the tradition of faith our pilgrimage is not a nameless wandering, a drift to nowhere. If God is above all our knowing, the tradition reminds us that the excess is of fullness rather than of emptiness. God lies in the direction of the greater rather than the less. God exceeds our knowing by abundance rather than by deficiency.

Irenaeus' aphorism, *Gloria Dei Vivens Homo,* contests every claim that God is somehow in competition with humankind. God in creating opts for life.[1] A reconsideration of the creation tradition shows that God is magnanimous and generous. Yves Congar rightly discerns the 'benignity' of God in creation and in re-creation. God's bestowal of life is a blessed gift rather than a poisoned chalice. God's glory is not served by human sacrifice of any kind. The biblical account of Abram's attempted sacrifice of Isaac shows this clearly: 'contrary to all kinds of other sacred powers, Abram's God did not want human life sacrificed to him'.[2] This interdiction of human sacrifice is a notable contribution of Hebrew faith. God's glory is never purchased by human diminishment. It is never to the cost of human development. Again, one stresses, God is the God of life, of flourishing, of liberation. And so, whenever repression is practised in the name of God, a blasphemy has taken place.

The continuation of Irenaeus' words is seldom given: the glory of humankind is the vision of God (*gloria hominis visio*

112

dei). Life is a project—a pilgrimage of which the definitive term is face-to-face communion with God. Despite the most unpromising circumstances we are never immersed in a straitjacket. Existence is not the sterile absurdity depicted by Beckett's *Waiting For Godot*. It is not a meaningless, pitiable *now* without hope or future. Irenaeus' reminder brings us closer to the Eastern Church's stress upon *theosis* (divinisation) and, indeed, to Teilhard de Chardin's conception of patterned movement towards Omega point. From the first gift of creation to the invitation to share the life of the Trinity, we encounter the graciousness of God, the diving goodwill which brings us to an intimacy with God hitherto unsuspected.

Yet, for many people, the threatening perception of God drives a wedge between their humane sensibilities and the possibility of their belief in God. As the Second Vatican Council avows, the practice of Christians has given ample cause for disillusion. Third world theologians gathered at Dar-es-Salaam bleakly remark: 'Theology for centuries did not seriously challenge the plunder of continents, and even the extermination of whole peoples and civilizations. The meaning of the message of the gospel was so blunted as not to be sensitive to the agony of whole races.'[3] We therefore return to the question of the masks of God. Or, perhaps better, we return to the delicate work of learning from both the tradition in which one stands and the tension felt whenever the tradition comes under critical question.

We must ask about every concept of God whether it is oppressive or liberating. Presentations of an alienating God are always to be contested as hindrances to knowledge of God. They are the pernicious outgrowths of vested social interest or of latent psychic mechanisms. The harshly primitive God drummed up in unexpected quarters from schoolroom to cathedral tells more about 'his' apologist than about the living God. Such a God is not more than an idol. Its foundation is repressed emotion, will to power or burning resentment. Again, the God of 'law and order' is a handy crutch for power-defending cliques. Latin American theologians of liberation have emphasised that oligarchic land owners and magnates of every kind enlist God to the chaplaincy of their causes. They generously bedeck God with the insignia of their interests:

security, anti-communism, defence of 'western' or 'Christian' civilisation. However, the God of these classes lacks one characteristic which marks out the living and true God: concern for the widow, the orphan, the oppressed and the victim. Since the God of Jesus Christ is bent upon the flourishing of creation, we must regard it as a duty to reject the masks which obscure God's intention for good rather than evil, for weal rather than woe.

The French theologian Jacques Pohier has argued that God is not everything: *Dieu n'est pas tout*. If God were everything then there would be room neither for love nor for freedom. Pohier's is a passionate, even anguished, cry for the autonomy necessary for all growth and flourishing. Without such autonomy creation itself would become oppressive. There must be 'space' where life and love can be lived and loved for themselves. We must have the freedom to relate to others not simply in God or in Christ but also for those others' own sake. We must have 'a space' to be alone with self where one is not overlooked or supervised. Pohier reminds us that Adam was alone before Eve's creation even though he was and remained the creature of God.

Does this not relegate God to the sidelines? Is it just another version of the Enlightenment's programme of self-sufficiency? Is it the *non-serviam* (I will not serve) of Milton's Satan. Not so. Rather, it insists that God's creative word is Amen. The 'let it be' of Genesis is close to the 'so be it' of every Amen. Creation is God's Amen to life. It is the bestowal of life, the most noble gift at God's disposal, short of divinising grace. From the creature's perspective, creation is indeed dependence. Yet, this is a relation in gift rather than in threat. God's creative gift facilitates growth, development and autonomy. In creation, God is like the good educator—communicative of self, yet allowing new growth in freedom. Fidelity to God's name makes it imperative to avoid all totalitarianism, whether psychological or metaphysical. God does not bind people with the chains of threat, authority, power or blandishment. According to St Thomas, God creates by supportive action. That support is by attraction more than by impulsion. God draws but does not drive. For people caught in a web of fear of God, whether through upbringing, education

114

or guilt, it is important to break that vicious hold. For them, it is all the more necessary to forsake the mask of God as proprietor of the universe or puppeteer or fearsome enigma. For them, it is of primary importance to reach for the appreciation of the gift of creation through the generosity of God.

There is the opposite danger. It is that one makes God out to be a cosmic 'beanbag'. All too easily we recast God to suit current fashion or to canonise our particular interests. In this direction, too, lies disaster. Such a God is the lethal figment of our desires. He/she/it is intellectually superfluous and ethically dangerous. We cannot recreate God to our own measure. *Our* best God is an idol. God must be allowed the first word. The most impressive attempts to reformulate expressions of God's nature and action quickly run to seed if they take on a life independent of the tradition. The many slogans of the late twentieth century—the God of meaning, the God of ultimate concern, the God of the utopian future—retain a Christian content only if they grow from and are kept close to the great tradition. A presentation of God must be more than a handy adaptation to the current intellectual fashion. Otherwise, it is little more than a variation of the God-of-the-gaps style. As a theological task it is imperative to keep in tandem respect for contemporary religious experience, attention to tradition's emphases in the theology of God and, finally, a critical estimation of the obstacles to the attainment of theological truth.

II

Creativity

The creativity of God is about the gift of being. Our existence, our powers, our being are not our own. They are received as a good gift to be cherished as such. To realise this is already to move towards thanksgiving, towards eucharist. It is to reflect on an entirely beneficient relationship. When St Thomas Aquinas speaks of a relation of dependence, he is not suggesting childishness or servility. He is rather speaking of possibility, of capacity to grow and develop. From this perspective one can consider the overbounding generosity of God as well as God's creative power. Power is an ambiguous concept. Our first thought is of the grasping, manipulative power of exploitative people and structures. But there is another kind of power. The power of the parent to give life. The power of the educator to enable the growth of self-disposition in the pupil. The power of the lover to call forth in the other a joy, an energy, hitherto unsuspected. This is a pale reflection of the creative power of God.

The Judaeo-Christian tradition affirms that God is the origin of all there is. God is the origin of heaven and earth, of animals and plants, of people. This tradition also asserts that the earth and all it contains is good, very good. All dualism, all splitting of reality into heaven and earth, spirit and matter, is thus avoided. A positive, trustful, optimistic, yet realistic vision of God and creation is retained. The inalienable dignity and inescapable responsibility of humankind as image of God is asserted. Man and woman are to be merciful stewards of the earth. They are to care for it diligently and constructively. Here is a challenge to respect for God, for personhood, and for the earth in all its rich diversity.

Is the God of Genesis—of the six-day creation and of the pleasure park called Paradise—not too small for the incredibly complex world disclosed by astrophysics and molecular biology? Does the vista opened up by evolution theory not render the biblical account of creation irrelevant, dispensable, even trivial. Is the God of traditional faith, creator of heaven and earth, for all 'his' majesty, not outflanked by the new physics? Certainly, our universe is far older, more complex, and more vast than anything within the ken of scripture or traditional Christianity. Archbishop Ussher's computation of the moment of creation in the year 4007 BC now makes us smile at the naïveté. Today we swallow without too much strain the suggestion that the earth we tread is up to five billion years old and that the universe we inhabit is from fifteen to twenty billion years of age. School children can speak of an ever-expanding universe where the distance between stars and nebulae increases at a dizzy rate. Far from our earth being the centre of the universe, it is but a small speck within a universe populated by billions of stars. Our universe is only one of many million.

At the level of microphysics there are other causes for

116

wonder. The infinitely small assails our received thought patterns just as dramatically as the infinitely great. Even the atom, that apparently basic unit which for long we thought indivisible, is itself a veritable universe of protons, neutrons and electrons. We now speak of quarks and leptons, themselves components of sub-atomic particles. Thus is upset the mechanical view of the universe as a fixed quantity of interactive particles open to prediction and control by scientific means. From the work of Werner Heisenberg and Nils Bohr has emerged the sheer contingency or lack of predictability of sub-atomic matter. The universe is not an inert stuff. It is startlingly alive. It has a freedom, a contingency, a mystery hitherto unsuspected. Old assumptions as to what makes sense, and what does not, burst asunder. Relativity theory makes us reconsider our limitations in understanding time, space, freedom, objectivity. In a real sense, theoretical physics brings us up against mystery just when we were tempted to agree with Laplace's claim to total predictability.[4]

One should also note the so-called anthropic principle. Formulated by Brandon Carter in 1974, this principle adverts to the narrow margin of hazard within which intelligent life could arise anywhere in the universe. If certain electromagnetic and gravitational constants did not lie within a narrow range of values, carbon would not have formed in the quantities required for carbon based life. Helium production would have been either too great or too little. The life of planetary systems would not have been sufficiently long to allow for the emergence of organic life. It is as if 'someone had finely tuned the values of the fundamental forces that bind the atom or generate solar systems with man in mind'.[5]

In his work, *A New Science of Life*, Rupert Sheldrake speaks of a formative causation operative throughout the universe.[6] Sheldrake presses beyond any explanation which would halt at molecular structure of movement. He speaks of a formative cause which directs the whole process of growth and development. There is something beyond mechanical and energetic factors if the operation of the biosphere is to make sense. And so Sheldrake speaks of a morphogenetic field, a causation of non-energetic kind, capable of accounting for the emergence and development of physical and biological forms.

There is question here of a thrust from the lower to the higher levels of being. Each lower level relates to and finds ultimate meaning in the next higher level. Clearly, Sheldrake is speaking of a newer form of purpose or goal.

Each of the above-mentioned considerations is no more than an hypothesis. None is above contestation. At most, these considerations point towards a richness, a complexity, a mystery, within our world, which has received little recognition from the narrow operation of nineteenth-century science. They call in question any glib assertion that science is somehow atheistic. They bring us up against the sheer complexity of the universe. Without exaggeration one can say that 'in the late twentieth century mystery is being rediscovered through scientific research'.[7]

None of the above-mentioned considerations is a 'proof' of God. Nor should they be made to dissect the act of creation. God cannot be equiparated to evolution or life force or formative causality. However, they can help a theology of God in a number of ways. The believer in a God of creativity may be tempted to make his/her picture of God too cosy, too small, too constrained. The biblical stories of seven days of creation and of the primal garden of Eden are bounded by the cosmology of their day. Even when we take these accounts as symbolic and not literal reportage we are in danger of narrowing our perspective to existential or historical concerns. While cosmology should not be central to our theology some attention to the 'new cosmology' is imperative. To speak of the God of men and women, of justice, of liberation, requires that at some point we face the metaphysical question. Unless we are to reduce God to the underpinning of psychological and social integration, we have to face the question of God's relation to the cosmological process. The God of people must also be the God of the Universe.

This type of consideration can bring us only a limited distance. It reassures us that the concept of creation is by no means an irrational one. It reinforces the perception that to disqualify the idea of creation is merely the outcome of a prejudice equivalent to religious fundamentalism. Thereafter, we have to face the question of absurdity or meaning, impersonality or personality at the heart of creation. Are we to say:

We are the children of Chaos, and the deep structure of change is decay. At root, there is only corruption and the unstemmable tide of chaos. Gone is purpose; all that is left is direction. This is the bleakness we have to accept as we peer deeply and dispassionately into the heart of the universe.[8]

But is not this as much a faith as ever was faith in the God of the Bible? Is it not a religion of a kind? To declare corruption the ultimate reality is itself the result of an intellectual jump over a gap in evidence. It is as much a *saltus intellectus* (intellectual leap) as any existentialist decision in the face of absurdity. On the other hand, assuming an openness to belief in God and an openness to consider God's creativity, we can be led to affirm a directive purpose which supports all life. We can have our minds opened to the depths of this purpose when we consider the magnitude of the universe, the diversity of its processes and the extent to which it eludes our comprehension. Once again we confront the *possibility* of affirming mystery. We no longer need to trade on the 'gaps' which remain at the interface of scientific questioning. These 'gaps' get ever fewer and ever smaller. The lesson of history is that appeal to the God of the gaps is bad theology. The God of the gaps makes little theological sense and becomes progressively redundant. The Christian believer in God will find himself/herself moved to affirm God as creatively active through the operation of the laws of life rather than through their temporary suspension.[9]

Enough has perhaps been said. Yet there is a counter argument within theology which should be noticed. The counter argument comes from certain types of existential theology. The theology of the Word seems to confine itself to existential decision. Casting aside all link with history, and *a fortiori* with a theology of nature, it rests on the narrow base of choice or decision in face of a 'word'. This is the case with fundamentalist theology. In a different way it is also the case with the theology of Rudolf Bultmann and Karl Barth. Their disqualification of the human as such, their lack of a positive estimation of the natural, leads to a rarefied conception of God. As Karl Adam pointed out, the outcome is atheism even though this result is unintended.[10]

119

More understandably, the several strands of liberation theology move directly to biblical evidence to support the claim, absolutely well-founded, that God opts for the poor, the victim and the oppressed. Here too it must be insisted that in the interests of liberation theology itself, a certain theory of God's relation to the world as *creator* has to be attempted. This is not the question of primary hermeneutical option. Liberation theologies make an adequate case for their option for the poor as a hermeneutical principle. Yet to speak credibly about the liberating God it is necessary to relate that God to the reality within which liberation, social and personal, operates. Part of that consideration must be the metaphysical question of the range, depth and finality of God's creative activity.

Here both the thomistic notion of transcendent causality and the emphasis in process theology on God's activity by attraction, can be helpful. Both have to do with the intimate, continuing operation of God on the levels of the microcosm and the macrocosm. Both have the flexibility to allow for newness and freedom within the sweep of a developing world. To affirm God's transcendent causality allows for the autonomy of nature. The autonomy of created agents remains. God does not intervene or interfere as the cosmic puppeteer. On the other hand, for one who holds to the creativity of God, this autonomy, this ordered complexity, this glimpsed-at but never fully understood finality, depends on the divine creativity. To remain sympathetic to process thinking will require considerable effort on the part of the traditional theologian. At certain points he/she will find it difficult to go all the way with process theology in its particular conception of the immanence of God. Yet, one can travel with its stress on God's creative empathy with all that God has made. Process thought valuably moves away from the idea of the 'cosmic architect', the 'world designer'. It accepts that God is the foundation of order. But it also underlines that God is the 'goad towards novelty'.[11]

God the Origin and Goal of the Experience of Transcendence

In every man, in every woman, there is the blessed capacity to transcend the limitations of time and place. Through imagination, memory and desire each man and woman can go beyond the boundaries of his/her immediate situation. In this sense 'walls do not a prison make nor iron bars a cage'. To the theological mind, the ability to transcend has an immense significance. Without quitting our context we can go both higher and deeper than that context. We can construct a utopian vision in such a way that the pressure of the imagined future ensures that the here and now does not limit all our energy and aspiration. Transcendence spells out our capacity to rise above every limitation to what we can imagine, aspire to and hope for. Emmanuel Levinas reminds us that transcendence means *trans-ascendere*: to rise above and beyond the boundaries of self-containment and self-preoccupation. A long tradition emphasises the value of self-transcendence in attaining some knowledge of God. *Scito teipsum* (know thyself) is not a programme for self-absorption. In truly knowing oneself one is driven beyond oneself. Augustine could say 'we cannot know God except by going beyond ourselves within ourselves'. The prayer *noverim me, noverim te* (May I know myself, may I know you) captures it well.[12] In true self-knowledge there is some knowledge of God, be it only in search and aspiration. There is a knowledge of longing and desire as real as any knowledge formulated in ideas and concepts. We can know more deeply in the obscurity of our search than in the clarity of what we have possessed or already mastered. How much more inspirational is Augustine's admission of defeat than the most learned, theological treatise: thou hast made us for thyself O God, and our hearts cannot rest content until they rest in thee. Again, St Thomas's development of the divine attributes is impressive. Yet at the centre of his treatment is the 'natural desire to know God'. Aquinas is certainly drawing attention here to the detached, disinterested, unrestricted desire to know. Even more is he pointing to a divine unease which pushes us beyond every partial attainment in knowledge, love and freedom. This unease is a reaching out, a searching for something or someone greater and more fulfilling than anything our own powers can attain. Many centuries later, that great student of the medieval tradition, Henri de Lubac, sees here a claim that in every man and woman there is an innate thirst for the face-to-face knowledge of God.

Every significant theological statement is at once about God and humankind. In speaking about God we speak about man/woman in one way or another. The converse is also true. Every significant statement about man and woman is also about God. Truly to know man/woman is to know something about God. This is one of the implications of the Judaeo-Christian stress upon man/woman as image of God. The question then arises as to how we know man/woman: can any more specific content be given to the claim that humankind is in the image and after the likeness of God. A cursory acquaintance with the tradition discloses several answers. The image of God in humankind is variously said to reside in the memory, the intelligence, the will, the conscience of each person. All these have been taken to provide a clue not only to the deeper knowledge of what it is to be a human being but to a foundational understanding of the mystery of God.

Through a lifetime, Karl Rahner, surely amongst the greatest theologians of the twentieth century, has investigated the implications of the human ability to know and love in freedom. The ability to push beyond every boundary set by imagination or concept or desire is a clue that these spiritual processes may rest on 'holy mystery', even God. Reflective people of diverse times and places have attempted to speak of this holy mystery in myth, in poetry, in metaphor and in symbol. It is our privilege, and our burden, to discern a surplus in every act of knowledge and every free choice. Rahner takes this much further. He argues that 'the personal history of the experience of self is in its total extent the history of the ultamate experience of God also'.[13] What then is this experience of self? It is an experience of depth. Rahner puts it thus: 'man always experiences more of himself at the non-thematic living of his life than he knows about himself...'.[14] This 'more' is disclosed by the horizon of infinite truth and good against which any particular truth or good is recognised as such.

There is a pre-conceptual knowledge deeper than all our science, philosophy and common sense. There is a generalised search for good prior to any particular desire or choice. In common with Augustine, Rahner would see this horizon and search as limitless. It stretches to very infinity. Every item of knowledge, even the sum total of all knowing, is surpassed by the extent of our questioning. Every object of choice, even the range of choices, is radically insufficient against the backdrop of the unquenchable thirst for good. For Rahner, this thirst is not a vacuum, a vague want. It is holy mystery. It underlies and supports our knowledge and love while surpassing these to an infinite degree. It is not available to direct grasp. It cannot be directly imagined, conceived or rendered in an idea.

Nevertheless, the idea of mystery is not mystery itself. Mystery is indirectly given through consciousness of any finite concept of object of desire. Although mystery is present immediately, it is grasped only through the mediation of partial knowledge and finite love. Rahner speaks of mediated immediacy of mystery. Much earlier, St Thomas spoke of implicit knowledge and love. In either case there is presence of Holy Mystery in the spiritual processes of every man and every woman.

This approach does not negate the traditional proofs for the existence of God. These proofs are, however, placed second to an experience of mystery which cannot be certified by syllogistic demonstration. The experience, termed by Rahner 'transcendental experience', is original, un-derivative, prior to every proof and every verification. It underlies and is evoked by particular experiences of knowledge, love and freedom. Hence, it cannot be separated out for analysis in abstraction from everyday experience in knowledge and love. Reflection on particular experiences indirectly discloses their ground which is co-experienced and co-affirmed. The ground of transcendental experience is none other than the living God. It is not surprising that Rahner accepts Tertullian's claim that the human spirit is naturally Christian. Nor is it strange that Rahner can write: 'A theoretical proof for the existence of God is only intended to mediate a reflexive awareness of the fact that man always and inevitably has to do with God in his intellectual and spiritual existence, whether he reflects upon it or not, and whether he freely accepts it or not.'[15]

For Rahner, then, the affirmation of God rests on neither extrinsic authority nor private revelation. It arises from the experience of every man and every woman as knowing and loving subjects. The experience cannot be evoked by command or by edict. Behind Rahner's somewhat tortuous argument lies an invitation to attend to a deeper experience available to all. On the other hand, transcendental experience in knowledge and love is neither eccentric nor anarchic. As individual experience it is unique to each person and it is precipitated by non-repeatable objects or events. Nevertheless, it bears a universal structure common to every person whose knowledge and freedom thrusts above and beyond every limited truth and good.

The Jewish philosopher, Emmanuel Levinas, has retained the same kind of stress on transcendence as revelatory of the Other. Whereas many people will want to name the Other 'God', Levinas refuses such a premature identification. Transcendence designates 'a relation with a reality infinitely different from my own reality yet without this distance destroying this relation and without this relation destroying this distance . . .'.[16] As human beings we are turned towards the 'elsewhere', the 'otherwise', and the 'other'. There is a desire for the other where 'the other metaphysically desired is not other like the bread I eat, the land in which I dwell, the landscape I contemplate . . .'.[17] The desire is not reducible to need. Need is satisfied by absorption of its object to oneself. The need for food is filled by the eating of bread. The need for drink is satiated by the taking of water. The need for self-affirmation can be met by self-projection. The desire for the other, however, is more radical. Beyond the hunger of the body, beyond the craving of the senses, beyond religious or moral needs, there is a desire which goes beyond satisfaction through gesture or caress or attainment. This desire Levinas terms metaphysical.

The distinction between metaphysical desire and the desire arising from need accents human autonomy *vis-à-vis* the other. Levinas extends this autonomy to the creature in its relation to the creator: 'It is certainly a great glory for the creator to have set up a being capable of atheism, a being which, without having been *causa sui*, has an independent view and word and is at home with itself.'[18] If there is a transcendence, a metaphysical thirst for the Other, this is not built upon spiritual poverty or fallenness or awareness of sin. This desire, this thirst, has an austerity, a selflessness not commonly associated with need. It respects the otherness of the Other (which it does not attempt to possess) in the Other's ungraspable quality.

Consonantly with his Jewish inheritance, Levinas affirms the invisibility of the Other. The Other is above our imagining, our concepts, our ideas. Hence, God is not attained by the usual avenues of a natural theology, viz. a theory of causality or morality or ontological participation. God is accessible in justice. Who does justice knows God. Hence, Levinas can say, 'Ethics is the spiritual optics.' And again: 'God rises to his superior and ultimate presence as correlative to the justice rendered unto men.' Rather than an analogy of being, there is an analogy of justice. The face of the other (*visage d'autrui*), particularly the face of the needy other, discloses the Other: 'The dimension of the divine opens forth from the human face.'[19] The proximity of the neighbour as widow, orphan and stranger becomes an inescapable moment in the revelation of an absolute presence. An absolute presence is shown forth in the demand made by destitution. The face of the needy other *does not* permit the luxury of speculation or neutrality. One either responds or denies. One does not remain untouched. There is an authority in the need of the other which invades our privacy. It engages our desire for the Other. In the response to the need of the other, the Other is either acknowledged or denied. In the positive response one answers a claim in justice: 'to recognise the Other is to recognise a hunger ... [it] is to give ... to the master, the Lord, him who approaches as 'you' in a dimension of height'.[20] The ethical correlation between my invaded privacy and the other is truly a metaphysics. However, it is not a metaphysics of causality (Aristotle) or of participation (Plato). It does not depend on what we establish by reasoning whether deductively or inductively: God is not at the end of a smart syllogism.

Rather, it is a metaphysics of relation and is constituted by ethical demand and ethical response.

This, then, is a transcendence understood in a way at once similar to and yet quite different from Rahner's. Like Rahner, Levinas refuses to afford any direct grasp of God. Every attempt to 'totalise' the Other is avoided and even rejected. Both men share a marked hesitancy to identify 'God'. However, there is also a difference in their respective approaches. Rahner appeals to a deduction from everyday experience in knowing and loving to the holy mystery which enables that experience. This analysis of personal experience is coherent with the traditional injunction, *scito teipsum*. Levinas, however, enjoins a look towards the other as the bearer of transcendence. The face of the other breaks open my self-sufficiency, my metaphysical atheism. Discourse is commenced. Response is elicited. In that response the Other is discerned. The absoluteness of the other evokes in my world the otherness of the Absolute.

IV

The coming God of history

History is as much about the present and the future as it is about the past. It shapes and is shaped by human existence. Since it concerns human beings, history is not a closed circuit devoid of freedom or creativity. Although shaped by past and present, the historical future remains open. It is still to be created through free, rational, human action. Meaning is neither given in advance nor pre-determined. It is not an unavoidable fate, an inexorable *moira* or destiny. The realisation that history is to be fashioned raises the theological question of whether and how God accompanies historical endeavour. Theology has today moved back from its exclusively ontological preoccupation. Western theology, in particular, has made the idea of God as subsistent being, *Ipsum Esse Subsistens*, a dominant feature of its approach. Many people would argue that in this way our understanding of God has been narrowed down and rendered lifeless. Hope in God who wills human salvation has been stunted. Faith in the compassionate self-giving God had been obscured. Love of the God in whom resides our blessedness has been made dry and arid. The God of ontology lacks the freedom of the God of the Bible. This God is in danger of death from immobility. 'He' is in danger of being choked by 'his' own perfection. In an often cited remark, Martin Heidegger warns that the enthronement of the god of western metaphysics initiated the modern banishment of God: 'Man can neither fall to his knees in awe nor can he play music and dance before this God.'[21]

When history is taken seriously as a place where God is known, there is a move away from the static, majestic and yet predictable God. While remaining the faithful, dependable God of the Old Testament, the God of history is also the God of surprise. God, in remaining the God of the fathers, Abraham, and Isaac and Jacob, is also the coming God of our descendants. The pull of the future, the hint of the undisclosed, becomes as important as emphasis on the past or preoccupation with the present. The search for God will not rest in visions or epiphanies here and now. It will not remain fixated on the present. Rather, with changeful intention it will enter the struggle to accomplish a perhaps unknown and undisclosed but hopefully better future.

Undoubtedly there is here a danger of flight into the future from an unpromising present. This would be both escapist and reactionary. It would also be a deformation of faith-under-standing of God. However, it is not an inevitable consequence of attention to the future. Christian hope is a vision which challenges present inhumaneness and seeks out an alternative order of things. Such utopian vision is far from alienating. Its attention to the future (with remembrance of past suffering) is both realistic and transformative in the present. Utopia releases the creative energy and the creative imagination required if the *status quo* is to be effectively challenged and overcome.

Some theologians prefer to speak of God as possibility (*posse*) rather than being (*esse*).[22] Thus they endorse the priority of the future over the present. The Irish philosopher, Richard Kearney, develops an analogy between ontological possibility (*posse ontologicum*) and religious Possibility (*Posse religiosum*).[23] One cannot define God into existence. Nor does

127

the substitution of a capital for a lower case 'p' make a theology. Nevertheless, there is an affinity between the concept of God as 'possibility' and the awakening of people to their own possibility for creating a more humane history. As distinct from the self-satisfied, infinitely complacent *Causa Sui*, the Bible images a God who accompanies the struggle for justice, who beckons from God's own future. Can we speak of the God who makes possible, who 'possibilises' the human future? This God is not simply the God of the indicative mood (what *is*) but is also the God of the conditional (what may and can be). Clearly we are moved towards the God who enables the ethical project of justice and love. This is the God who wills justice, who favours the poor and the victim, who is mysteriously but really present wherever there is love.

We are led to think of the God of eschatology. New possibilities reside both 'within' being and beyond it. A distinction can be made between the *futurus* and the *adventurus*.[24] The *adventurus* connotes the element of otherness. It cannot be subsumed in the present. It retains its liberty. It carries the ingredient of gratuity, something over and above the intrinsic capability of created being. Here one thinks of the biblical promise that God, through God's free gratuitous power, will raise up the dead. Those who sleep in the dust of the earth will rise to eternal glory. So too will those who are beaten down and oppressed here and now. The *Deus adveniens* both vindicates the dead and enables a transformative hope amongst those deprived of any human future.

The *Deus adveniens*—the *adventurus*—is heralded by anticipations in the here and now. In the midst of unresolved suffering, in apparent chaos and absurdity, precursors of the coming God are given. Glimpses of another order are caught. Clues are discerned to an alternative scheme of things. The embodiment of the kingdom of God in Jesus is the best example we have. It exemplified an alternative mode of existence where all would be sons and daughters of the same Father. This kingdom cannot be inaugurated by human power. The labour of the cross was required to provide the setting for the inbreak of the kingdom at Easter and Pentecost. Similarly, we struggle in small victories and great defeats to keep open to God's future. At the time of writing one is moved by the courage and dignity of the Birmingham Six. Even as they were remitted to a continuation of their unjust and prolonged imprisonment not a word of bitterness escaped their lips. Whoever reads the writings of Richard McIlkenny will be struck by their hold on God in numbness, grief and defeat. Again there are the unforgettable words of forgiveness uttered by the sorrowing father whose daugher was taken in the Enniskillen bombing. The refusal of bitterness, the hope in her blessedness, surely evidence a power that comes from beyond human capacity and, indeed, from beyond the grave. By means such as these, creative imagination for service of the kingdom of justice, love and peace is kept alive. Along this path of pain, of courage, of hopeful service to the truth, people may discern not the exact features but rather the traces of who God may be. Along this path of pain and courage, God's future is built in so far as it can be built by human endeavour.

God's future with its roots in the present is not a purely abstract fancy without impact on the present. Rightly are we suspicious of a future ever deferred. God cannot be relegated to the innocuous future. Faith in the coming God must relate to the present in order to challenge it and there to lay the seeds of something greater. Where the coming God is taken seriously the lure of sacred places and institutions is not allowed to predominate. The shrine and the temple with their custodians and hierarchs notoriously attempt to imprison God. However, the coming God, the *Deus Adventurus*, whose action stretches from first things (protology) to last things (eschatology) will not permit such entrapment.

The coming God is not forgetful of the past

The hope for the future, rooted in the coming God, must be allowed to retain its full range. There must be a future for the nameless dead. There must be a hope also for the vanquished and the slain. Paul expresses it well: 'those who are alive shall not precede those who have died'.[25] It has been pointed out that the bias of historical studies is frequently dismissive of the conquered. History is the story of the winners. It seems to shout, 'Woe to the losers' (*vae victis*). For this reason it is important that theology be also 'a kind of anti-history ... out of the memory of suffering—an understanding of history in which the vanquished and destroyed alternatives are also taken into account'.[26] There is a valuable protest in favour of the dead in that particle of the creed: 'I believe in the resurrection of the dead'. It expresses a solidarity with the 'suffering of our forefathers'. The dead also have a future. This affirmation arises out of hope, hope in the coming God. It also stems from a justice of the spirit as indispensable as justice in distribution of material goods. The insistence upon God as the hope of the dead has a socio-critical importance. It keeps alive 'the memory of the suffering that has accumulated in history in order . . . to determine our behaviour and our hopes'.[27]

The memory of suffering (*memoria passionis*), understood as the awareness of the suffering of the ages, can prevent our speech about God from becoming flabby and complacent. This disturbing memory keeps alive a bias of protest against suffering caused by the strong and the powerful. It provides a direction for vision and hope, preventing such vision from becoming vague, cliché-ridden and supportive of the *status quo*. It seeks out the traces of the coming God, traces already indicative that God vindicates all who have suffered and died without redress. This is not a new version of pie-in-the-sky-when-you-die. Rather, it provides a motivation for human action which will be just to the living and solicitious for the dead.

Nevertheless, it is God—and not any person, group, party or class—who is the subject of history. The meaning of history resides in God's freedom. Claims to institute a final or Messianic age come under serious question. Such claims are untrue to reality, betray human possibility and discount its victims as expendable. They also proclaim 'woe to the vanquished' (*vae victis*) and 'hail Victor' (*salve victor*). The God of the future, disclosed in the self-giving love of Jesus Christ speaks to us from the past and out of solidarity with all suffering. The future proclaimed is not a creature of the right or of the left. Remembering this self-giving kenotic love we have 'a narrative remembrance of the triumph of failure'.[28] The future it discloses includes those who have been discounted by the prevailing utopias. It includes the victims of history, the conquered in all wars, those who died without name or trace. J. B. Metz rightly insists that 'the political meaning of our history does not depend only on the survivors, the successful and those who make it'.[29] This meaning looks beyond all human utopias. It looks to the God who raises up the fallen, vindicates the suffering and—in God's own freedom and time—institutes the full victory over our tortuous history of human suffering.

We do not meet God face to face. We meet God through men and women in the struggle to put an end to unmerited suffering and to build a healed, healthy, happy life not merely for ourselves but for all people. This kind of knowledge looks both to the past and to the future. In a sense, for the Christian the great symbol of God is found in the past: 'the future [of God] ... has already commenced in Jesus as the Christ.'[30] In another sense the future opened up by the life, death and resurrection of Jesus is the great symbol of God. For the believer, God is present in our remembrance of past happenings —Exodus, Covenant, Paschal Mystery, the Gift of the Spirit. God is also present in the demand of the moment, particularly that of sacrificial love. Finally, God is present to our expectations that God will carry out new surprising *magnalia*. The hiddenness of God in this very presence is underscored by the fragility of all our doing. The incompleteness of all our projects questions the illusory claims of a theology of glory. God is ever ahead of us even while fully with us. God remains the God of surprises.

Theism Revisited. A Presence in Absence

I

Deus semper maior (God is always greater)

What do *you* mean by God? At first hearing, this is a super-fluous question. Do we not all recognise the word God whether in loving acceptance, hostile rejection or bored indifference. Yet there is the rub. 'God' means very many things. 'God' means different things to different people. And so in speaking of God people appeal to prefabricated allusions from text books and dictionaries—ruler of the universe, object of supreme adoration, Lord of all. Or else, and this is the harder task, one confronts one's own belief/unbelief with its aspirations and uncertainties, its hopes and fears, its evasions and its complexes. Who follows this path discovers that 'God' is a composite idea made up to a disconcerting extent of one's own mental bric-à-brac and inherited socio-cultural assumptions.

Our ideas of God do not drop down from heaven. They are partly made up of our communal and personal yearnings. Again, they are fashioned by psychological forces lying deep in our psyche. They are strained through childhood influences. They arise from the deposit of our culture which even as it rejects God yet persists in fashioning its own god-language and its own god-images. Above all, our ideas of God come through the religious tradition into which most of us were born. This adds up to an interplay between each individual and his/her tradition.

The finest minds in the Judaeo-Christian tradition stress that God, to be God, remains beyond all that we can know. The memory is there of a God who refused to yield up the divine name, preferring to be known as I am who I am or I am who I will be. That reticence is seen in the Jewish unwillingness to pronounce the divine name or to set up any images which might take from the hiddenness of God. Henri de Lubac reminds us that one should not presume too quickly to name the living God. For whoever controls the name all too easily entertains the illusion of controlling the One behind the name.

And so, for Christianity, God remains above our words, our concepts and our judgments. Neither our thought nor our expression can capture God. At best we catch glimpses or clues which we take to point to the God ever ahead of us. From Augustine to Aquinas, this theme is taken up in different ways. Augustine indulges his love for paradox in the following lines:

> cum absens putatur, videtur;
> cum praesens est, non videtur.[1]

Augustine also writes:

> Deus qui melius nesciendo scitur.[2]

This is not the vacuum of ignorance. It is the presentiment that God remains ever greater than our best knowing. If Church fathers like Augustine, Chrysostom and Novatian stress the importance of a *docta ignorantia* it is because of their feel for the greatness of God who cannot be bounded by our words and ideas. God inhabits light inaccessible. This is an agnosticism of a kind. Yet, it is a *reverent* agnosticism. St Thomas Aquinas gives us a clue to its meaning. Several times he reiterates that we best know God when we know that God is above all our knowing. In this he simply repeats a centuries-old tradition. He also distinquishes between our way of signifying (*modus significandi*) and the thing signified (*res significata*). Our way of signifying is always marked by the limitations of our own experience and knowledge. Our ideas remain limited. Our images remain fractured. Our words remain halting. Yet, for Aquinas, in and through these very ideas, images and words we grope in the right direction. We avoid tailing into inconsequence. Here there is an interplay of affirmation and denial. Having uttered the affirmation of our tradition and/or our rational reflection we have immediately to deny that God can be cast even in the most careful affirmation. Yet on that denial there follows a further affirmation. It is in the more rather than the less that the reality of God lies. Thus we grope towards the light rather than the darkness. John Courtney Murray puts it with customary elegance: 'Along this way of affirmation and negation all the resources of language, as of thought, must be exploited until they are exhausted. Only then may man confess his ignorance and have recourse to silence. But this ignorance is knowledge as this silence is itself a language—the language of adoration.'[3]

This principle of negation-within-affirmation prevents our theology, our speech about God, from hardening into idolatry or softening into verbosity. It frees us to face new questions, to move from old positions where these are seen to be untenable. To change the metaphor, this principle enables us to entertain ever new 'masks' of God, which may themselves be destined to be replaced at other times and in other circumstances. We are helped to avoid making absolute any of our images of God. Thereby we are helped to respect the divine mystery.

Is God a person? That God is a person seems clearly affirmed in Judaism, in Islam and in Christianity. For Jewish and Christian traditions our belief, our devotion and our prayer centre upon God as a 'Thou' who listens, who is receptive to prayer and worship, who is to be loved, served, honoured and adored. The personal pronoun 'he' has enjoyed uncontested usage until recently. People address God as 'Thou' in prayer and in liturgy. It is one of the great joys of many people to address God as Father and to say that the definitive revelation of God is in Jesus Christ.

However, there are difficulties. 'Person' normally denotes individual human being. The concept is inseparable from the changeableness, the limitations and the foibles of our humanity. J. G. Fichte pointed out that 'person' implies limitation and finiteness. To say that God is a person, without further corrective, can lead to the image of the patriarch, the venerable elder or some such. At worst, it conjures up the figure of harshness and severity that has haunted the consciousness of so many people. Short of this, it can reduce God to human dimensions and confine people to an infantile stage of faith and practice.

Yet, Christian tradition is nuanced in the affirmation that

God is a person. Christians confess that God, while one, is also three. Here the understanding of personhood is different from the normal definition. Again, there is a long tradition in mystical theology which speaks of a 'God beyond God'. The tradition presses beyond any simple notion of person. Thus, to offer an example, the Irish monk and scholar, Eriugena, could write 'Only this definition can be predicated of God, that he is "he who is more than being".'[4] These qualifications do not imply that God is impersonal. They do not imply that God is sub-personal, a vague life-force, an amorphous *élan vital*. Nothing could be further from the meaning of the great mystics or theologians. They simply apply the principle already noticed—*Deus semper maior.* God is not a person in the limiting sense of personhood. Yet God realises or includes all that is perfect in personal being. Here Aquinas supplies us with a valuable clue. In his *Summa Theologiae* he argues that since personhood is what is most perfect in all of nature it is fitting that personhood should be predicated of God.[5] Aquinas has in mind attributes such as freedom, self-disposition, the ability to know and love. These are predicable of God *eminentiori modo* with the proviso that such attributions give us no purchase for the trivialisation of God. Rather they impel us to see God as the one who is supremely living, supremely loving, supremely compassionate.

God, then, is not one person amongst others. For that would set a limit to God in the way one finite person limits another. Again, God is not *a* person. In the Christian confession, God is three persons—Father, Son and Holy Spirit. It is better, therefore, to say that God is personal in a supreme and inimitable way. God must be thought of in terms of freedom, self-disposition and untrammelled initiative. To use personalist terms, God is subject rather than object. God is fully *sui compos.* As personal subject, God can enter relationships with other personal subjects in knowledge and love. This relationship is creative. It enables every created existent to live, move, and have being. God's pershonhod is not over and against the creature. Rather it is constitutive of every creature.

Only a God who is personal subject can have a name. Only a God who is personal subject can give fidelity and demand loyalty. Only a God who is personal subject can be more than a vague generality or a lifeless symbol. Address from such a God evokes the deepest faith, hope, love and devotion. A mark of the biblical concept of God is that it sees men/women as partners of God in dialogue. Man/Woman is addressed by God and is endowed with the capacity to make personal answer. In freedom and love, indeed in rejection and disobedience, man/woman can return the word of God's address. The books of the Pentateuch, the Psalms, the book of Job, show how man/woman can enter a living conversation with God. The God of the Bible prefers man/woman to stand erect and talk—as did Job with extraordinary frankness, as did Moses for all his stammering.

II

The Theist Affirmative in Old and New Testaments

As mentioned earlier in this study, the strict monotheism of the Old Testament may have emerged as late as the seventh century BC. There is some evidence that earlier worship of Yahweh did not contest the validity of the worship of other gods by other peoples. After the reform of King Josiah (641-609 BC) there is an impassioned proclamation of both the uniqueness and unicity of God. The Yahweh-alone movement represented by Jeremiah and Deutero-Isaiah emphasises the uniqueness of God: the Lord is God; there is no other besides (Deut. 4:35; Deut. 6:5). The unicity of God finds expression in the protestation of the consistency and trustworthiness of God's enduring love, as we saw in chapter 3. One finds this in Hosea, Jeremiah and Deutero-Isaiah to an outstanding degree. Other attributes are equally affirmed. The holiness, the justice and, indeed, the wrathfulness of God are frequently detailed in the Old Testament. With the creation-salvation theme of Deutero-Isaiah and Genesis (in its final form dating from the fifth century BC) the transcendence of God to all creation is powerfully confessed. Yahweh is truly personal in promise, in covenant and in sanction. Despite the constant avowal of the otherness of Yahweh, whom no-one can see and yet live, the Old Testament predicates human-like attributes to God: anger, pleasure, love, concern, readiness to punish and reward.

There is, therefore, a constant interplay between the hidden-ness and the presence of God. On the one hand the Old Testament says 'truly thou art a hidden God'. On the other hand, the same Testament ascribes everyday roles to Yahweh as shepherd, king, general of armies etc. Such usage can give the impression that Yahweh is like 'the touchy, vain, imperious tyrants who ruled the empires of the world'.[6]

The New Testament view of God is as original as the fact of Jesus Christ is new. There is continuity here but also an immense development—just as Jesus Christ himself stands within the Old Testament tradition while stretching it to unforeseen limits. The shape of God's salvific intent is discerned anew. Jesus' own consciousness is of God as loving Father, a caring and compassionate Abba. In the preaching of Jesus the attributes of mercy, of concern for the poor, of a wide-ranging compassion, shed a softer light on the somewhat stern, though by no means exclusively stern, presentation of the Old Testament. The overarching symbol of the kingdom of God takes on a new resonance in Jesus' preaching and parabolic teaching. As Jesus presents it, the kingdom symbol affords a powerful impetus to action for justice, mercy, brotherhood/sisterhood, truth and love. The statement 'The kingdom of heaven is like . . . ' leads to the injunction 'Go thou and do in like manner.'

The life, death, resurrection of Jesus evoked a specifically new realisation—that God is Father, Son and Spirit. The shape of God's intention is discerned in startling freshness in the work of Jesus of Nazareth. Karl Rahner reminds us that New Testament teaching does not offer a philosophy of the attributes of God. Rather it details the *attitudes* of a personal God as these are shown forth in the ministry of Jesus.[7] God is a God of love whose loving kindness has been enfleshed in Jesus Christ. The most decisive announcement of the New Testament is that God—the Father—has called us to a familial community as adopted sons/daughters in Jesus and through the power of the Holy Spirit. Clearly, the focus of the new apprehension of God's deed is the life-work of Jesus experienced by his intimates during his lifetime and reflected upon in the church community after his death.

In its overall development the New Testament represents an

expansion of the concept of God. Yet it also retains the Old Testament's insistence on the one-ness of God and on the service of God as a task daily to be renewed. God is the cause of all; in God all things live, move and have being; this God is not far from each of us; gives life and breath to all.[8] In his epistle to the Romans, Paul affirms a knowledge of God which in principle is open to all through their intelligence and their conscience. The monotheism of the New Testament is strict despite its readiness to confess Father, Son and Spirit. In his article 'Theos in the New Testament', Karl Rahner formulates this helpfully:

> In this alone can it become apparent whether the one God is really God, and indeed the unique God for those who confess him. They must have no idols by the side of God, neither Mammon, nor the belly, neither statues nor forces of the cosmos, neither local rulers nor the emperor in Rome.[9]

As a reflective theory, the theist affirmative is not elaborated in the preaching of Jesus. Jesus enjoined a practice rather than a theory. Nevertheless, the concern of Christians to find consistency between the biblical faith and the questions which occurred to critically minded people soon gave rise to detailed reflection. Dating from the irruption of Christianity upon the Graeco-Roman world, an intermingling of biblical and philosophical thought categories became inevitable. John's logos-theology and Paul's creation-theology try to show the cohesion of the cosmic and the kerygmatic aspects of the new faith. Through the eternal word of God the world was made. yet, this word has come among us to be seen, heard and touched.

Throughout a tradition of nearly 2,000 years, from Paul to Augustine, from Aquinas to Teilhard de Chardin, Christian theism has striven conceptually to hold in unity the creative action of God and the divine economy of salvation. The platonic idea of the One and the Aristotelian notion of being were used skilfully by Augustine and Aquinas in different ways to provide a rational underpinning for belief in God. While neither thinker would dream of reducing the affirmation of God to the outcome of speculation, both shared a vigorous

138

confidence in the ability of reason to think through, in order to deepen, a prior commitment to God. It would be mean-minded and ungenerous to deny the achievement of their efforts. They tried to show that, far from damaging our intelligence, faith in God was the flowering of the thrust of the human spirit to know truth and embrace good.

III

The Critique of Theism

Nevertheless, the theist affirmation has come under considerable pressure. Perhaps the most dramatic example of this is the 'death of God' theology. Among mainstream theologians strong criticism is also advanced. Dietrich Bonhoeffer criticises the kind of religion which keeps people in fear before an alienating God. Mature faith must be able to live as if God did not exist: *etsi Deus non daretur.* Paul Tillich welcomes the demise of the God who appears 'as the invisible tyrant, the being in contrast with whom all other things are without freedom and subjectivity'.[10] J. A. T. Robinson speaks of the displacement effect of theism. Robinson's metaphor is taken from mapmaking where every projection has the effect of displacement or distortion as one approaches the edges. Theism is a projection. It is an attempt to utter the unutterable. In trying to speak about mystery it projects God as the great 'over and against', the 'out there now' or some such. Its displacement-effect is to invent a God who is an object apart from the universe, an 'absentee entity'.[11] According to the process theologians John Cobb and David Griffin, there are five traits to the God of classical theism. Such a God is conceived of as (i) cosmic moralist (ii) who is passionless and unchanging (iii) who is supreme power (iv) who sanctions the *status quo* (v) who is dominant male.

For many, such a God has become morally intolerable. For many others such a God is a distortion of the God of Jesus Christ. This God risks becoming a hateful monster. 'He' is a being of whom are predicated absolute being, impregnable self-sufficiency and eternal impassibility. But, it is argued, a God who cannot suffer is a God who cannot love. Such a God is poorer than any man. If love implies some openness to suffering and if God cannot 'feel' this suffering then God cannot really love. An apathetic God—who cannot feel with or experience real compassion—leaves us to our misery. 'He' remains eternally self-absorbed, a *Deus incurvatus in se.* When one adds to this picture the universe of suffering within creation one is driven to protest. Thus emerges the contemporary depiction of God as despot, even as sadist. All atheism of protest should be set against this background.

IV

Theism Revisited

Patriarch Maximos IV could say, 'The God the atheists don't believe in is a God I don't believe in either.' One can say this only if one is prepared to revisit theism. One must be prepared to face the alienating features of all our masks of God. Are we prepared to step back from presenting God as the policeman of morals, the supporter of the *status quo*, the distant ruler long in power and short in compassion? Will we admit the displacement effect of theism and allow that the unmoved mover, the transcendent creator, are models which call for supplement. We may rightly insist that these have their value. We may refuse to follow those who, from Pascal to Barth, have driven a wedge between the God of reason and the God of faith. Nonetheless, we have also to remember that the best efforts of traditional theism have led us no further than Rudolph Otto's *mysterium tremendum et fascinosum.* The divine mystery is indeed 'tremendous' and 'fascinating' but it can also induce fearful paralysis while seeming to remain impervious to the pain of the world. One is driven willy-nilly to conceive of an inaccessible despot whose favour must be courted and whose wrath is to be feared.

One approach to rethinking theism is pantheism. Pantheism tends to link God and world in such a way that God is said to be everything and everything is said to be God. Mystical in tendency, it is disposed to identify nature and history with the outworking of God's developing selfhood. Baruch Spinoza (1632–1677), the best-known of modern pantheists, can speak of *Deus sive natura* (God or nature). Nature, according to Spinoza, is a particular way God exists. Consciousness is a particular way God thinks. G. W. F. Hegel (1770–1831) seemed to regard history as the development of the divine idea through the dialectic of thesis, antithesis and synthesis. Hegel casts the divine mind as the one all-encompassing reality, at the cost of the freedom of creation and the otherness of God. Perhaps it is fair neither to Spinoza nor Hegel to regard them as confusing God with nature or history. Yet the pantheist failure to respect the otherness of God to the world is unsatisfactory from the point of view of Judaeo-Christianity. It is also unsatisfactory from the standpoint of a critical philosophy. In taking the sensible world seriously and attributing to it divine-like characteristics—as many forms of pantheism do—it appears to confuse God with nature. In taking spirit seriously—as many forms of pantheism do—it appears to make the world a film or veil of the divine. With considerable point, John Macquarrie has argued that pantheism tends to collapse into either athestic materialism or unworldly spiritualism.[12] Pantheism is, therefore, hardly an acceptable revisitation of theism.

Well short of pantheism is another tradition noticeable in the writings of the mystics although not confined to them. It holds that God while remaining other can receive all things into Godself. Pan-entheism emphasises *not* that God is all things but that all things are in God. God remains God. Creation retains its relative autonomy. Yet it subsists in the divine personal field which sustains it and enters a real relation with it. This view stands between theism (in its stern transcendence) and pantheism (in its tendency to confuse God and the universe). Panentheism affirms the existence of God as a personal other. It also emphasises that the world matters to God in a positive way. Rather than envisage any kind of static, non-mutual relationship between God and God's creation, it speaks of a dynamic relation whereby all reality resonates to the supportive activity of God. Visible creation presents a new challenge to reverence and responsibility, not because it is God, but because it is present to God. The term 'panentheism' was framed in the nineteenth century by Karl Kraus, a disciple of Hegel. It is equivalently broached by some of the late medieval mystics as well as by Eriugena, the Irish scholar, and by Nicholas Cusanus, polymath and cardinal of the Roman Catholic Church. One can argue that Teilhard de Chardin adopts certain of its main positions while J. A. T. Robinson devotes considerable space in his works to expanding the idea. Teilhard de Chardin repeatedly criticised the view of God as the 'neolithic proprietor of the universe', aloof and unconcerned with the wellbeing of people and things. In a careful way he moves towards panentheism when in his *Mass on the World* he writes:

> like the pagan I worship a God who can be touched; and I do indeed touch him over the whole surface and in the depths of that world of matter which confines me: but to take hold of him as I would wish I must go always on and on through and beyond each undertaking, unable to rest in anything, borne onwards at each moment by creatures and at each moment going beyond them, in a continuing welcoming of them and a continual detachment from them.[13]

However, there is also a problem here. The very term 'panentheism' seems to veer towards pantheism with all its unacceptable overtones. God appears to be some kind of cosmic force, impersonal and even sub-personal. An example of this is J. A. T. Robinson's reference to a 'divine-field'.[14] As the text cited from Chardin hints, there is a danger of a quietist mysticism whereby the importance of human endeavour in changeful action for the betterment of the world is played down. This was not the intention of either Teilhard de Chardin or Bishop Robinson. It does not follow from their positions and it does not necessarily follow from panentheism when carefully thought through.

'Dialectical Theism'

In his Gifford lectures, John Macquarrie introduces the term 'dialectical theism'. This valuable work—*In Search of Deity*—takes up with sympathy the long tradition in mystical and scholastic theology which issues in a systematic yet critical theism. God cannot be defined even by our best efforts—*Deus*

142

definiri nequit. Yet it is incumbent to bring together what is said of God in the biblical witness, in religious and secular experience, and in critical reflection. Macquarrie takes issue with the refusal to consider any avenue to knowledge of God other than the biblical revelation. Thus he questions Blaise Pascal's and Karl Barth's dichotomy between the God of the Philosophers and the God of the Bible. Yet Macquarrie is open to a certain dialectic of affirmation. He presents a series of antitheses in the hope of reaching a more nuanced theism. In speaking of God we have to proceed dialectically. Our every affirmation is balanced by a counter-affirmation. And from that apparent incoherence can emerge a less unsatisfactory approach to the uncaptured truth. One *must* speak of God as being—lest one appear to deny the reality of God. One must speak of God as non-being—lest one appear to enmesh God as one being amongst others. In the same way, one speaks of the unity and multiplicity of God—lest, on the one hand, one reduce God to polytheism or, on the other hand, overlook the richness of the life of the Trinity. One speaks of the knowability of God and yet of God's incomprehensibility. One has to speak of the impassibility and yet of the passibility of the compassionate God. One must speak of the eternity and the temporality of God. And one has to speak of the transcendence as well as the immanence of God. Each couplet, and each member of each couplet, says something that has to be affirmed of God. In their mutual tension they correct the deficiencies of each affirmation taken on its own.

This dialectical theism with its sympathy for both transcendence and immanence offers good hope for a helpful critique of the 'masks of God'. It enables us to respect the mainstream of theism while maintaining a critical reserve towards every affirmation or negation in regard to God's attitudes or nature. Such reserve is part of the reminder that God cannot be adequately described. It is also part of yet another dialectical critique, viz. of tradition as both gift and threat. For the Christian the biblical images and the rich content of the Judaeo-Christian tradition have offered the most useful avenue to relationship with the living God. Yet every image and every doctrine carries its negative underside. Even the God of justice can seem to conflict with the God of compassion.

143

The Lord of Hosts, the Holy of Holies, can induce a paralysis before a *potentia absoluta* (absolute power).

V

God's mediated immediacy

Today, there is widespread experience of the absence of God. In the post-Enlightenment West, God is experienced as an enigma if not an absence. The surveys of opinion in Ireland as elsewhere show a steady increase amongst those who profess 'no religion'. For some, this represents an emancipation from old superstition. Such emancipation is welcomed as an opportunity to deal with the social, economic and political problems which beset us. The silence of God, it is said, provides a space for men and women to speak constructively, effectively and autonomously. Others, however, will argue that the banishment of God is a destructive illusion. The silence of God, a culturally imposed silence, leads—they would say—to the death of humanity. In their view, it is imperative that the voice of God still be heard, that the work of God still continue. With Karl Rahner, they will say that on the day the word 'God' dies, on that day too humankind dies. Between both views there is a wide terrain for debate on the meaning of secularisation as well as on its achievements and failures. For those who believe that God still speaks, it is necessary to examine critically their own conceptions of God's presence. In doing so they must try to avoid abstraction, presumption and premature certainty. In accounting for our hope in the presence of God, we must respect both the hiddenness of God and the concreteness of that presence. A task of this kind presupposes close attention to the great biblical symbols of God and the retention of our philosophical nerve. Capitulation in either direction leads to a fabricated idol subordinate to our vested interests or to the monstrous deity of fundamentalism.

The person of religious faith will want to affirm that God is immediately present. With Augustine, he or she will confess that God is present with a greater intimacy than the most intimate experience of self. *Deus intimior intimo meo.* This is more than a psychological experience. It expresses our apprehension of creation as a relation of gift. From God we live, move and have being. Creation mediates a presence. God is present creatively and supportively to all God has made. God's creative presence is such that it enables the creature to be both dependent and free. We can act as if God did not exist (*etsi Deus non daretur*). Nevertheless, we remain beholden to God for life, movement and being. This beholdance is neither a burden nor a debt. It arises from a divine presence which lies deeper than anything we can directly touch or experience. How, then, is the immediate presence of God known. It is known in mediations which disclose God even though they are not identical with God. As Christians we may claim an immediate relation to God in creation and recreation, in nature and in grace. Yet we have also to say that we have no direct hold upon God. God's presence, though very real, is always elusive. The Old Testament rightly stresses that we cannot see God face to face. God remains beyond our grasp. God may be discerned by the eye of faith but always through a glass darkly. In somewhat paradoxical terms we can say that God is known in mediated immediacy. God touches us immediately. Yet we can know of this only through mediations. No-one has ever seen God. Nor does God hand out letters of credence signed and sealed. For the man or woman of faith God indeed speaks but always indirectly. God speaks in the experience of our creaturehood and of our adoptive sonship/daughterhood, in people, in events and even in things. This mediated immediacy is 'the gateway through which God enters our history through which we can ourselves really perceive God and can express him in words'.[15]

It is important to be clear on this. God is not met as an object among others. That would domesticate God as the property of hierarchies and mandarin classes. God could then be constrained by sacred places, times and formulae. Such, however, is not the God of Exodus, of the covenant, or of Jesus Christ. The true God remains ever free of all these constraints. The basic presence of God is the relationship of creation—'a mutal relationship between the finite person and his absolute origin, the infinite God'.[16] However, if we are to know this, we must have the mediation of an experience or disclosure. The primary mediation of God's immediate presence is the experience of our createdness. This is not the experience of an architect, artificer or planner. It is the experience, rather, of being centred by a creative Centre, of being empowered by enabling Power.

Thereafter, the privileged mediation of God is, for the Christian, Jesus of Nazareth. In him, for the Christian, God is mediated in attitude, word, deed and history. The pattern of Jesus' life, in so far as this is discerned by critical scholarship and remembered in Christianity, shows how humankind might walk with God and how God wishes to walk with humankind. The courtesy of Jesus, his care for the weak, his labour for the kingdom of simplicity, hope and love, provide clues of the disposition of Jesus' Father. His parables expand our own perception of God at once gently and radically. And yet, it is not just a matter of knowledge. God is present in Jesus in word, in will and in action. Here God's history is to be found. Here God shows God's true countenance to Christians 'in the unselfish involvement of Jesus as the good shepherd'.[17] Christ is truly *the* sacrament of encounter with God. If this is taken seriously, a reconsideration of our conception of God is required. God is to be found in the earthly history of Jesus Christ. What does it mean to say that the closing hours of Jesus' life on earth disclose, in mediated immediacy, the deepest presence of God in this world? To answer, one must take both cross and resurrection with utmost seriousness.

The cross of Jesus can be taken as the place of the silence of God. Once can understand the words placed on the lips of Jesus—'My God, my God, why hast thou forsaken me'—as his protest at abandonment by the Father whom he trusted. There is some merit to this understanding. It prevents our forgetting that Golgotha was a crucifixion not simply of Jesus' flesh but also of his faith and hope. On the cross the self-emptying of Jesus reached its most costly point. Despised and rejected, he experienced the hiddenness of God at its most impenetrable.

And yet, we must avoid a quasi-existentialist preoccupation with the seeming absurdity of Calvary. There is much more to it than the cult of resignation or of suffering. It is not a melo-dramatic instance of the silence of God, although it has much to say to those who experience that silence. For the Christian the cross is a climactic instance of the mediated immediacy of

God. Through his death on the cross Jesus enters solidarity with executed slaves, with criminals and with the victims of all times. This is effectively shown in the Latin American representation of the 'Christ of the Indies'.[18] There, the broken, tortured, crucified Christ has neither beauty nor grace. In this representation is only the naked, ugly cry of pain. This Jesus, this Christ, does not withdraw from but rather enters fully into the opprobrium, the pain and the shame which has been heaped upon the losers of all ages and places. Whoever believes in Jesus as the crucified holy one of God can indeed say that God speaks in the pain of those who suffer. This is the shape of the compassionate presence of God. It is also the most available evidence to the Christian that God is with the victim, the sufferer, the defeated ones of history.

We can say this only if we say that Jesus is the Christ. And we can say that Jesus is the Christ only if we hold to the Easter vindication of the crucified servant of God. The reality of Good Friday and of Easter is a unity. The vindication of Jesus is an action of God which touches the history of all people. It is the great instance of the presence of God to the world in and through Jesus of Nazareth.

Here God is not the distant other of the theology of paradox. Nor is God the oriental potentate, the slave-owning, alienating omnipotence criticised by Simone Weil.[19] The God disclosed to Easter faith is not selfish, complacent, uncaring of the well-being of God's children. On the contrary, this God is present wherever people suffer. The Father of Jesus Christ is involved with the sufferer and comes to meet him/her from a totally new future. The significance of Easter for our conception of God is immense. Easter discloses to the eye of faith that God is the power of self-giving weakness. Easter signals the triumph of failure, the strength of self-giving love, the hope of the faltering. This is neither the theology of God's suffering nor the diminution of the power of God.

It is, however, a radical reconsideration of the idea of power. Evangelical power is not the same as domination or force or control. Evangelical power, discerned in Easter, is the effective presence of God in life, death and the vindication of the dead. This presence of God in the history of Jesus is not limited to one moment in time. Jesus died for our sins and was raised for our justification (Rom. 4:25). Through his Spirit, that self-emptying yet triumphant love continues. In the power of the Spirit Easter penetrates the whole of creation. Creation and recreation form an intrinsic unity. Paul's words are memorable: all creation has been groaning for the redemption of the children of God. The power of Easter, kept alive through the Holy Spirit, is at work in God's whole creation. Suffering vindicated by God lights up a creation which would otherwise be doomed to futility. If we can see the imprint of death and resurrection throughout all life then we can also see God differently. God is seen to be at work in an Easter way whenever creaturehood is lived out authentically. Just as Jesus' Easter mediated the immediacy of God so too do the lives, sufferings, achievement and death of all God's children mediate the hidden yet real presence of God.

Jesus' inclusion of the outcast, his freedom in regard to establishments of all kinds, his death through the collusion of civil and ecclesiastical rulers, his vindication even in the midst of failure, represent both a strong headline and a motive of hope for all who would follow his 'way'. They also tell us as much as we can know about the nature of his Father and ours. If exclusive and selfish establishments put Jesus to death we have ample reason for saying that exclusive, selfish and established patterns of behaviour are unlikely to mediate the immediacy of God. Rather, God is more likely shown forth wherever the pattern of Jesus' life work is reiterated. The hope of a pilgrim people, gathered in the memory of Jesus, is that a pattern, proportioned to our own times and places, of Christ-like action can be maintained. Jesus cannot be imitated any more than any other figures of history can be imitated. However, his pattern of justice, his care for the least of things, his compassion, and his witness to the kingdom of God can be for those who attempt to follow him a continued mediation of God in ever new immediacy. This will be neither more nor less than living by the great disclosure symbols incarnate in Jesus of Nazareth: service of the kingdom of God, life in the presence of a compassionate universally concerned Father, and hope in the vindication of all in the new heaven and the new earth. If we take the life, death and resurrection of Jesus to be the privileged mediation of God's immediate presence, our

148

imaging and speaking of God will be rooted in the style of Jesus of Nazareth. And if we place his teaching and doing in the context of the hope of Israel, with its pattern of promise and surprising outcome, our speech about God will be at once concrete and yet tentative.

We cannot read off the mystery of God from a finished blueprint. Any such pretension runs counter to both Old and New Testaments. The hiddenness of God remains an attribute of God. Every self-confident attempt to intrude on that mystery is an empty pretention. On the other hand, even if we cannot penetrate the being of God, we can learn from the action of God in our midst. God is not separate from God's works. The great deeds of God preached in the early Church allow us just enough clues to keep us in faith, hope and love. They allow us to know God in remembrance and in anticipation. They do not enable us to capture or tie God down. The God of creation and the God of Easter is the God of *Ex-hodos* (going out). As in the liberation of the Hebrews, God does not remain in light inaccessible, complacent of suffering and distress. God is an outgoing God whose Exodus is for the blessedness of people and of creation. God is the God of practical love. The disclosure of Jesus' Father remains in the giving of the cup of cold water, in the daily carrying of the cross, in the worldly yet very sacred service of the neighbour.

Facile optimism is always a cruel delusion. It may comfort those already comfortable but it leaves the sufferer in his/her pain and isolation. For the tradition of Israel, suffering—particularly unmerited suffering—remains always a scandal. It was an unresolved question dogging the affirmation of God. As Elie Wiesel pointed out, the Jew regarded it as his/her right to remonstrate with God on the ground of innocent suffering.[20] Our modern experience must render us sensible to the accumulation of grievous suffering. Despite the official histories written with a victor's hand and dismissive of the suffering of the losers, we must try continuously to give voice to the suppressed stories of the victim. In the midst of violence perpetrated by institutions and structures ridden with greed, selfishness and terror, one will have to ask, 'Where is God here?' With the best of Jewish and Christian writing we can claim that God is present even in unredeemed conditions. God is not present only in the beautiful and serene. God is also present in the ugly and the tormented. God can be experienced in the night of darkness. God can be invoked in suffering and adversity. Even though the invocation be a tormented protest, it can be both effective prayer and good theology. Conversely, we have the right to utter the name of God only when we are ready to enter solidarity with the suffering. Perhaps, our unwillingness to enter this solidarity is the reason why our speech about God has become jaded and unconvincing. Walter Brueggemann writes: 'It is likely that our theological problem in the church is that our gospel is a story believed, shaped and transmitted by the dispossessed; and we are now a church of possessors for whom the rhetoric of the dispossessed is offensive and their promise is irrelevant. And we are left to see if it is possible for us again to embrace solidarity with the dispossessed.'[21]

To give an account of the hope within us is the most impressive kind of theology at our disposal. Hope is never pure theory. It retains an open-endedness which overturns pure theory. It reshapes itself in the light of both disappointment and attainment. It is therefore a pilgrimage which relies upon the God of pilgrims. Christian hope looks forward through the prism of a continual dying and rising. There is the daily death of failure, disappointment, frustration and boredom. There is the daily rising, prayed for when we ask that our daily bread be given, of refusal to capitulate to hopelessness, abandonment of faith or denial of love. A truly theological word will convince us that in this our death and rising, God is present. Not as a postulate or make-believe but in mediated yet very real immediacy. The inevitable factor of bodily death, our own and others, colours our hope. Here again we respond to God's presence both by realistic acceptance of the inevitability of death, and by persevering refusal to allow it the last word.

We are moved towards a new, yet very old, affirmation of God, a God who becomes present in our action and whose purposes can be blocked by our refusals great and small. The practice instituted by Jesus in the service of God's kingdom, the brotherhood/sisterhood inaugurated in the eucharist, the seeds of eternity contained in every act of justice and love, mediate God to us really yet indirectly. We must not place

God 'too high or too far away'. Rather, God is within us, around us, about us and above us. In *The Great Hunger*, Patrick Kavanagh discerns the presence of God:

> ... in the bits and pieces of every day
> —a kiss here, and a laugh again, and sometimes tears,
> a pearl necklace around the neck of poverty

To explore the inner depths of God is pretentious and misleading. *Deus in se* (God in God's self) lies beyond the reach of our knowing. *Deus pro nobis* (God for us) is disclosed in many ways of mediated immediacy. St Thomas Aquinas laid constant stress on the relational quality of our knowledge of God. We do not know *what* God is. We may know *that* God is. Thereafter we must rely on the relations established by God with us. However, we dare to believe that God is not different from what such relations disclose. While we know only in part, we believe that God is not different from what has been given in our experience of Christ and in his accompanying Spirit. The God who is always greater than our furthest knowing can nonetheless be truly known even in the least of things.

9

In the End, God–Father, Son and Blessed Spirit

'The question about God and the question about
suffering are a joint, a common question.
And they only find a common answer. Either that or
neither of them finds a satisfactory answer at all.'
J. Moltmann[1]

I

God and the problem of evil

The grim fact of suffering is indisputable. In nature and
history it bestrides our existence. The long story of innocent
suffering, the accumulation of senseless pain, has driven many
to describe their world as a cursed blight. Secular protest
movements derive their nobility from refusal to acquiesce in
the structures of pain, deprivation and exploitation. Religious
faith at its best also contests unjust suffering. It aspires to an
alternative, better order of things. In both secular and religious
terms, therefore, the appropriate *first* reaction in face of
suffering is resistance to the utmost of one's powers. Before we
analyse suffering—or, for that matter, evil—we must utter a
clear NO to them. The rounded phrases of theoretical analyses
can obscure the scandal of unmerited suffering.

Just as everything healing and good is borne by tradition so
too the conduit of much suffering and evil is that same
tradition. As host for the structures of injustice, tradition
can harbour patterns of domination and repression. When
protest at human-made suffering bursts forth, it frequently

rejects tradition as the carrier of pain and injustice. Such protest frequently rejects the idea of God, itself fashioned by tradition. To contest unmerited suffering is often to declare the absence or the indifference or the impotence of God.

Protest is by no means confined to atheism. The 'wandering Jew'—afflicted by persecution yet full of faith—recurrently asks if God has ever been clearly on the side of the oppressed. What anguished faith lies in the Psalmist's cry 'How long, O Lord, How long'. The same question has arisen from many a sick bed, at the graveside of a beloved parent or spouse or child, from the desolation of a prison cell, from the steps of the gallows, from before a firing squad. In these circumstances, it is understandable that the God who is said to be benevolent, provident and omnipotent should be charged with dereliction of due care. If we speak of the God of the widow and the orphan grim experience at times mocks our words. Where was God in Auschwitz? Where is God when cancer strikes? When famine rides it awful gallop? Some will ask: Is God impotent? Unconcerned? Malign? For Albert Camus the only response is metaphysical rebellion. Ivan Karamazov's words may spring to other lips—'it is not God that I do not accept, but the world he has created. I do not accept God's world and I refuse to accept it.'[2]

One response is to attempt a defence or justification of God. The discipline of theodicy (*Theos* = God; *Dike* = justice) faces the question austerely formulated by David Hume: 'Is he willing to prevent evil, but not able? then he is impotent. Is he able, but not willing? then he is malevolent. Is he both able and willing? Whence then is evil?'[3] It is imperative to note the pitfalls attending this kind of enterprise. All too easily it demolishes a straw man while leaving real suffering unnamed and unchallenged. Much classical theodicy works from an abstract concept of evil. It considers not suffering, injustice and deprivation but rather an acontextual reconstruction of evil. Standing in academic detachment, it shrinks from the risk of involvement. It overlooks the cost of solidarity with the sufferer. Forgetting the situatedness of all knowledge it can end by obscuring the demand of practical resistance.

A pilgrim's theology must travel with those who suffer. It must attempt to feel their anger and remain sensitive to their pain. If it does not, it will merit the criticism articulated by Hugo Meynell: 'For the very reason that these men do not weep, there is something unsatisfactory about their rejoicing.'[4] Yet compassion is not the same as sentiment. Any worthwhile theology must retain a critical edge even when it comes to the searing fact of evil and to the inescapable onrush of suffering. Otherwise, it will lean towards one or other form of existentialist indignation. Indignation alone is insufficient. It is not enough to bewail an evil world and an uncaring God. The element of transformative hope is necessary in order to motivate work for change in face of suffering.

Perhaps the first distinction to make is between pain and suffering, on the one hand, and evil, on the other. Pain and suffering frequently *are* evil. Yet they are neither necessarily nor always so. Pain and suffering are an integral part of life itself. Austin Farrer has argued that pain as such needs no justification: 'Pain, being the grip of a harm the creature has failed to shun, enforces the heed that was lacking or evokes the effort that was unexerted.'[5] Somewhat similarly, Herbert McCabe reminds us that 'If pain were unnecessary for our survival we should long ago have discarded it like our tails'.[6] The *fact* of pain and suffering does not disprove either the goodness or the power or the concern of God.

Immediately it must be said that pain and suffering do not always carry this relatively benign form. There is an appalling surplus of pain in nature and human experience. Nature is indeed red in tooth and claw. There is animal and human pain. People suffer cruelly and inexplicably. Random illness strikes without regard to virtue or innocence. Here once more there is room for distinction. In an evolving world there is an attrition to all physical interaction which leads to both decline and development. With customary directness St Thomas Aquinas argues that if there were no corruption there would be no generation. New life springs from very death. The process of nourishment takes a toll in the vegetative and animal domain. The cancer which wreaks so much havoc is the operation of a self-contained system. If we are part of an evolving world we cannot hope to avoid all set-back and shock from that world's processes. Can there be a world like ours without suffering, pain and death? Transposed into theological

154

terms this question may be answered by Farrer's tough-minded argument: 'God is the God of hawks no less than of sparrows, of microbe no less than men. He saves his creatures by creating in them the power to meet the ever-changing hostilities of their environment. And so, though individuals perish and species die out, there is a world of life.'[7] These considerations are in no sense a defence of pain or suffering. It is rather to say (a) that pain and suffering are not identical with evil and (b) that in a world where the very process of development includes maturation, senescence and death, 'the pain and agony of the world is just what you would expect to find in a material world—no more and no less'.[8] In the natural world, that is to say, the scientifically explicable world—pain and suffering have a 'natural' cause. They are the negative side of some good and are susceptible of scientific explanation.

In the case of beings who can exercise freedom, i.e. a choice determined neither in specification (choosing this rather than that) nor in act (one could have refrained from choice), the categories of good and evil take on a particular meaning. Some would argue—as does C. Tresmontant—that it is only with conscious beings that good and evil are applicable categories. In this view evil first emerges with consciousness. At the pre-conscious level atrophy and deterioration cannot be termed evil. Evil is whatever diminishes individual or personal existence. Physical evil is then injury, illness, death. Moral evil is injustice, oppression, exploitation, cruelty. Moral evil is corrosion of minds and emotions through deprivation of stability, hope, personal integrity. Moral evil is sin—the abuse of freedom whereby God's love is placed second to an idol. Moral evil cumulates in its effects to become an incubus on human existence. It casts a pall over countless lives and effects a lethal combination of suffering, pain and alienation. It is clear that suffering, pain and death as we know them are not unaffected by moral evil—itself the outgrowth of freedom's abuse.

The classical theological view of evil is that it is a privation rather than a positive thing. Evil is defined as *privatio boni debiti:* it is the absence of a good which ought to be there. Lack of vision in a human being is an evil. In a stone, it is not an evil. Yet evil is more than an emptiness. It is a real disorder at the

155

heart of being. Evil is, as it were, parasitic on good. For St Thomas Aquinas every act, every event, every process, is good precisely as being. Evil lies in the perversion of good. In this way, classical theology exculpates God of the creation of evil. God has given being. All being, as being, is good. Moral evil is the abuse of freedom carrying effects which are both physical and moral. All other pain and suffering, for the classical tradition, are the obverse side of processes which in themselves are good. At a stroke, the classical tradition appears to have exculpated God and to have rejected Gnosticism with its emphasis on a second 'god' originative of evil.

Clearly the classical theological tradition—represented by Aquinas and Augustine—insists that God is not the cause of evil. God cannot be the originator of evil—otherwise, there would be evil in God and God could not be all-good. Alongside this, the classical tradition holds that God allows things to go wrong and failure to occur. There remains, therefore, a difficulty. One cannot claim that God allows creatures—either through their own legitimate operation or through abuse of God-given power—to cause pain, suffering and evil and at the same time say that God has nothing to do with these effects. At the very least, we have to say that God permits evil. Is God, then, not implicated in pain, evil and suffering?

Here again, the classical tradition is somewhat tough-minded. It admits that God is the cause—albeit indirect (per consequentiam)—of evil. God allows or permits evil to occur. St Thomas makes the point that God acts for the best 'on the whole' (quod melius est in toto) not for what is best in every single instance. For Aquinas, then, in God's disposition (and in nature's disposition) the good of the whole comes before the good of each part. Here one has to agree with a very sympathetic commentator of St Thomas, F. C. Copleston, that 'this picture of God as a kind of artist and the universe as a work of art, requiring shadows as well as light, is apt, in spite of its traditional character, to appear disconcerting and unhelpful to many minds'.[9]

Implicit in the classical argument is that in our world the possibility of some pain and evil is inevitable. St Thomas will argue that where beings can fall short of the good some of them will in fact do so. Where there is freedom there will be abuse of it. Alien as it sounds to our ears, Aquinas can say that much good would be precluded if evil were not permitted. For the classical tradition, therefore, God both permits moral evil and, in creating the kind of physical world we inhabit, indirectly causes physical evil. Thus arises Aquinas's paradoxical claim that if evil *is*, God *is—si malum est, Deus est.* This is surely an audacious claim. It represents the very reversal of the modern statement: since evil is, God is not. St Thomas, however, would say: 'If there were no God there could be no good; if there were no good, there could be no evil. But there is evil. Therefore, there exist both good and God.'[10]

Yet the question remains. Is such a God morally tolerable? Is the God who foresaw and yet permitted the accumulation of basic sin, moral evil and appalling suffering a monster and no God? In reply it is variously argued that God permits evil that good may come of it, that injustice and oppression have their sting drawn in the triumph over them by justice and love. Thus the Easter liturgy proclaims: 'O happy fault ... which gained for us so great a Redeemer.' We have already alluded to the argument that if God makes people free, God 'must' permit the misuse of freedom. Some would say that it is a nonsense to speak of creatures free to choose good or evil who were nonetheless precluded from the choice of evil. In the context of purely rational argument this approach is minimally helpful. It is vulnerable to Anthony Flew's dry comment: 'To call such a being, ruthlessly paying an enormous price in evil means to attain his own good ends, himself good, is mere flattery.'[11]

The argument from free will is not quite so open to attack. Notice that the traditional approach does not claim that freedom is outside the ambit of God's causality. Even our free acts are performed under the aegis of God's enabling causality. Thereafter, the classical argument is that the value of a world wherein freedom exists—and can be abused—outweighs the evil of the abuse. That God allows such an abuse evidences, it is argued, God's forbearance, powerfulness and love rather than unconcern. This argument has little force unless it is backed up by a commitment to action for humane development and by resistance to unjust suffering. Neither Judaism nor Christianity have ever claimed that we have the best of all possible worlds. In both traditions, and in their combined thrust, man and woman are regarded as called to combat evil—in themselves, in the structures they fashion and in the history they create. We are called to make our world a more humane and fraternal/sororal place. This is not to evade the difficulty raised against the goodness and omnipotence of God. It is rather to argue that God's omnipotence is best seen in God's respect for our freedom, God's love best seen in God's ever present grace and help. Our world is surely one in which evil is rampant. In large part the evil is attributable to human wrong doing. All the more urgent, therefore is the call to practical love in combatting sin, injustice and oppression whether these come from ourselves or from others.

II

The Passion Of God

Thus far can theodicy bring us. To pursue it any further risks either acquiescing in pain and evil or restraining protest at unmerited suffering. Suffering can defy all explanation. And evil has a monstrous quality, a malign absurdity. Walter Kasper's claim that theodicy is the question on which both theism and atheism founder is, therefore, entirely comprehensible.[12] A pilgrim's theology must avoid that ultimate contradiction—justifying the unjustifiable and domesticating evil by abstract and comfortably vicarious explanation. Can there be an innocence in face of unmerited suffering? Hardly: 'in face of suffering you are either with the victim or the executioner …'.[13] Suffering raises an urgent imperative to compassion. One of the imperatives of a pilgrim's theology is to insist on raising the question of God's compassion. Is God capable of compassion? Does God enter solidarity with suffering? In what way is the compassion of God shown? What does this tell us about God? What does it tell us about suffering?

Abraham Heschel speaks of the theology of God's pathos. One *must* speak of God's capacity to suffer. An unconcerned, immovable God is not the God of Israel. For prophetic faith, God suffers. Events, actions and sufferings in history really affect God. Both creation and covenant are God's risk. They entail God's creative involvement with the world and God's historic involvement with the people of the covenant. Here, even for God, there is risk—the risk of love. There is vulnerability here—the vulnerability of love. God's suffering is the passion of creative love (creation) and of loving loyalty (covenant). Rabbinic theology insists on the *pathos* of God. The rabbis envisaged the self-humiliation of God—in creation, in covenant, in exodus, in exile. In the exile, the compassion of God is discerned by prophet first and later by rabbi. God accompanies the people into exile, grieves with them in their grief and suffers with them in their suffering. For that reason rabbinic theology can refer without strain to pain in God.[14]

In the Christian tradition the passibility (capacity to suffer) of God is recurrently affirmed. Early patristic theology can speak of the benignity and humanity of God. Ignatius of Antioch can argue that 'The timeless and invisible one became visible for our sake; the incomprehensible and impassible one became capable of suffering for our sake'. Tertullian speaks of a *Deus Mortuus* (dead God) and of a *Deus Crucifixus* (crucified God). The boldest of all of these, Origen of Alexandria, entertains the idea that God can suffer with the suffering of love—'First he suffered, then he came down. What was the suffering he accepted for us? The suffering of love.'[15]

The most memorable contemporary suggestion that God's compassion involves the suffering of God is from Elie Wiesel's study, *Night*. This much discussed passage is represented here as a powerful formulation of God's passion with the victim:

> One day when we came back from work, we saw three gallows rearing up in the assembly place, three black crows. Roll call. SS all round us machine guns trained: the traditional ceremony. Three victims in chains—one of them ... the sad eyed angel ... all eyes were on the child. He was lividly pale, almost calm, biting his lips. The gallows threw its shadow over him ...
>
> The three victims mounted together onto the chairs.
> The three necks were placed at the same moment within the nooses.
> 'Long live liberty' cried the two adults.
> But the child was silent.
> 'Where is God? Where is he?' someone behind me asked.

159

At a sign from the head of the camp, the three chairs tipped over. Total silence throughout the camp. On the horizon the sun was setting.

'Bare your heads' yelled the head of the camp. His voice was raucous. We were weeping.

'Cover your heads.' Then the march past began. The two adults were no longer alive. Their tongues hung swollen, blue tinged. But the third rope was still moving; being so light, the child was still alive...

For more than half an hour he stayed there, struggling between life and death, dying in slow agony under our eyes and we had to look him full in the face. He was still alive when I passed in front of him. His tongue was still red. His eyes were not yet glazed.

Behind me, I heard the same man asking:

'Where is God now?'

And I heard a voice within me answer him:

'Where is He? Here He is—He is hanging here on this gallows...'[16]

The affirmation of God's presence on the gallows comes from Wiesel's Jewish heritage. It is neither a metaphysics nor some cheap apologia fashioned at a safe distance. It does not attempt an exculpation of God—a divine defendant can hardly be acquitted. Least of all is it a justification of suffering. Wiesel's affirmation is crafted *within* suffering. Here one sufferer addresses another about the absence and presence of God. Coming from solidarity with the victims of Auschwitz, Wiesel's testimony is filled with the memory of suffering. This is a *shekinah*-theology, a theology of the divine indwelling. Whereas priestly theology saw God's presence in temple and in worship, this affirms God's presence on the gallows, gibbets and crosses of all times. God is present in a suffering way. Such theology neither adulates suffering nor enjoins masochism. It affirms the power of God in suffering and the strength of God in weakness. Above all it affirms hope against hope that God is with the victim, in suffering, despair and death.

Our century gives ample evidence that history is rarely in black and white. The distinction between the victim and the executioner can become blurred. The victim sometimes plays the executioner against yet other victims. The human tragedy is that in all of us there is the capacity to be victim, executioner and detached, though guilty, spectator. Elie Wiesel puts it thus:

> Deep down, I thought, man is not only an executioner, not only a victim, not only a spectator: he is all three at once.[17]

Here is a reminder that no one can confidently arrogate God to his/her side. There is always the possibility that in becoming executioner or spectator one has forfeited the *shekinah*, the divine presence. For that same reason we should be slow to 'christianise' Wiesel's gibbet-parable. J. B. Metz warns against harnessing the pain of others to one's case for God. Who really has the right to answer the god-question which arises in suffering? Who can say that God is here—on this sick-bed, on this gallows, in this prison, at this graveside? Judaism, Christianity—indeed all faith in God—are questioned by the incident related in Wiesel's story. Premature apologias are insensitive, even incredible. Faith has to *struggle* towards the discovery of God in suffering. It cannot do so by hi-jacking the pain of others thus robbing their memory of its disturbing rebuke. The most credible affirmation comes from him or her who experiences that place 'where God and humankind, full of terror, look into each other's eyes'.[18]

III

What Does Impassibility Mean?

A theology practised with an awareness of suffering is forced to reconsider its imaging of God. In face of suffering, it must reconsider the claim that God cannot suffer. The traditional affirmation of God's *apatheia* (incapacity to suffer or change) has to be re-examined. For many this affirmation—of a God who cannot suffer with the suffering—has become problematic if not scandalous.

Yet, the classical affirmation of God's impassibility has a positive core. Or, to be more precise, it becomes positive in negating a negative. It denies that God can be changeable or fickle. It denies that God can be manipulated by rites, wizardry or magic. Thereby it differentiates God from mythical deities capriciously responsive to charms and spells and incantations. The claim that God is impassible affirms the freedom of God and thus God's ability to free others. St Thomas Aquinas remarks 'To bewail [*tristari de*] the misery of others does not appertain to God, but it does most properly appertain to God to dispel that misery.'[19] Impassibility, therefore, is not the same as unconcern. The claim that God can neither suffer nor change safeguards both the dependability of God and the autonomy of creatures. God is not buffeted by history's flux. Therefore, God can be relied upon as a firm support. The impassibility of God is really about God's reliability: 'I the Lord change not: therefore you, sons of Jacob, are not consumed.' (Mal. 3:6) In this way too, history is freed from the capricious rule of the gods. History is seen to be entrusted to human effort and care. God does us the compliment of entrusting to us the development and stewardship of the creation given into our care.

Yet the *apatheia* principle has been misused. All too frequently it has been made to support the prevailing models of God as distant ruler, judge or monarch. As if to say, a worthwhile God must always have absolute control. Or again, a vulnerable God must be defective.[20] One must ask can such an understanding allow for God's sympathy with pain, suffering and defeat, not to speak of God's entry into them. Does it not project our own fear of failure, of vulnerability, of deviation from the respectable norm? Is it not the reflection of our need for security? Perhaps we still hanker after comfortable servitude to a supreme, omnipotent authority. All too easily, the invulnerable God plays into the hands of the strong, the powerful and the successful who are only too happy to buttress their own position thereby. The impassible God becomes the ideological ally of dominant forces in society: the generals, the rulers, the mighty of the earth.

Can we affirm at once the impassibility of God and the compassion of God? Christian faith makes it incumbent on us to affirm both. The sense of the faithful (*sensus fidelium*) recoils from any view of God as unconcerned and invulnerable. Here is where metaphysical theism is seen to be insufficient:

for theism, God cannot suffer and yet remain God. Here, too, is where mythology discloses its own insufficiency: in mythology, god is one agent amongst many. It is the merit of Jewish and Christian faith to press its thought on the unchangeability and the compassion of God through to a reconciliation in the love and the self-emptying of God.

Origen can speak of God's suffering through strongest love. Augustine can emphasise the weakness of God which is due, however, to the fullness of God's power. Both Origen and Augustine speak from the background of trinitarian under-standing. To affirm at the same time the impassibility and the compassion of God requires a move from the ahistorical God who rules in solitary glory. Jewish theology with its perception of God's accompaniment of the people in joy and sorrow, in success and failure, distinguished between God and God's presence-in-the-world (*Shekinah*). To cite J. Moltmann's memorable phrase, God's presence 'wanders with Israel through the dust of the streets and hangs on the gallows in Auschwitz'.[21] Rabbinic theology, without retreating from faith in the one, only God, nevertheless speaks of a dual personality in God. It speaks of God (who remains changeless as the ages) and God's indwelling presence (which can suffer human injustice and wickedness alongside the suffering and the persecuted). It affirms that God reigns in Heaven and yet dwells with widows and orphans: '...the one who is high...encounters men and women in what is small and despised...'[22]

IV

The Trinitarian History of God

All that is best in contemporary theology insists on a trinitarian—not tritheist—understanding of God. Correctly Jürgen Moltmann insists that: 'The doctrine of the Trinity is no longer an...impractical speculation about God, but is nothing other than a shorter version of the passion narrative of Christ in its significance for the eschatological freedom of faith and the life of oppressed nature'.[23]

Knowledge of the triune God is not derived from the

philosophy of theism. It arises from the structure of Christian experience of the *magnalia Dei*, 'the great deeds of God', manifested in Christ's life/death/resurrection and continued in our lives through the outpouring of God's blessed Spirit. Karl Rahner puts it well 'God's relationship to us is three-fold'.[24] We should neither deny nor exaggerate the classical distinction of the immanent Trinity (*Trinitas in se*) and the economic Trinity (*Trinitas pro nobis*). The immanent Trinity is the Trinity of the economy and vice versa. However, we come to know the Trinity economically or in historic stages—through the life-work of Jesus of Nazareth and through the movement he initiated.

As the fullest sacrament of God, Jesus is the definitive revelation of God's being and nature. All that has been said in this study about the parables of Jesus, his Abba sayings, his inauguration of the Kingdom, his death and his resurrection, must be reiterated here. These tell us who God is. They communicate what God wishes to be for us. Now, however, a further step is taken. All these elements of Jesus' life-work must be understood in a trinitarian context. We misunderstand Jesus' significance if we halt either at a biography of Jesus of Nazareth or on the threshold of simple theism. Jesus' life, death and resurrection bring us much further. They lead us into the very heart of trinitarian understanding of God.

There is ample reason to view Calvary as the triumph of failure. Ostensibly Calvary contradicted Jesus' preaching of God's Kingdom. To all appearances, it nullified his trust in the gracious presence of his Father. Calvary epitomised the onslaught of human malevolence and the outcome of freedom's abuse. And yet, Christian faith proclaims that on the cross the incarnation of God reaches its true meaning and purpose. Here Christ's self-giving love reaches its utmost expression. Here the Father receives back all that he had given up to the buffeting of the world's abuse. Finally, here the blessed Spirit is poured out on the world and on the Church. Thus, our alternatives are clear; to view Calvary as the failure of a good man or to see it as a trinitarian event which commences a new history. If we accept the latter alternative, we are driven to consider Jesus' death as the starting point for understanding the Trinity.[25] Calvary is where the fullness of

God's love is revealed in this world of suffering and sin.

The more we understand the cross as part of God's history the more our concept of God must become trinitarian. We must take account of God's historic involvement with suffering. Perhaps the most striking reference to this history is the self-emptying or *kenosis* attributed to Christ, the Son of God:

> His state was divine,
> yet he did not cling
> to his equality with God
> but emptied himself
> to assume the condition of a slave...
>   (Phil. 2:6 et seq.).

This text links God's historic involvement to the ministry and death of Jesus. Without diminution of divinity, God can enter the human condition to share its suffering and its brokenness. Here is divine self-giving. Here is divine sympathy. Here is God's suffering alongside the most rejected and the most afflicted. A temptation of later theology has been to limit this suffering to the human nature of Jesus: as if to say that it was the man Jesus who was obedient 'even unto death' while the second person of the Trinity stood aloof and untouched. Such an understanding hardly takes account of God's love present in redemptive suffering. If the fullness of God's love in redemptive suffering is taken seriously the limitation to the suffering of Jesus as man is transcended. We come to see the necessity for a trinitarian understanding of God's kenotic history—the trinitarian story of the divine self-emptying.

The word *paradidonai*—to deliver or give up—is used in the New Testament of both Father and Son. The word expresses at once divine initiative and divine sacrificial cost. For Paul, the Father did not spare his only son but gave him up for us all. Let us not overlook the emphasis upon the cost to the Father—it is the costly gift of love. If God was in Christ to reconcile the world (2 Cor. 5:19) such reconciliation was effected through the blood of the cross (Col. 1:20). The giving up of the Son represents the pain of the Father. We can dare to say as does Jürgen Moltmann, 'the Son suffers dying, the Father suffers the

165

death of the Son'. May we not also say that there can be suffering in God?[26] To 'give up' is also ascribed to Jesus. Paul speaks of the son of God—Jesus—'who loved me and gave himself up for me' (Gal. 2:21). The giving up, then, appertains to both Father and Son. Can we not say, *must* we not say, that two persons of the Trinity are involved in this self-giving drama of love that is the cross of Christ? Calvary does not concern only the divine and human natures of Jesus. Nor is it about propitiating the God of strict monotheism. It is a trinitarian event in which Father, Son and Spirit touch—and are touched by—our broken creation through involvement with the extreme reaches of its suffering.

The Gospel according to John sees the outpouring of the Spirit as taking place from the cross of Jesus: 'Jesus bowed his head and handed over the Spirit' (Jn 19:30). For John, Jesus' hour of glory—of suffering love—is also the hour of the Spirit. This spirit is the unitive force of the Father's sacrificial 'giving up' (*paradidonai*) and the Son's 'giving up' (*paradidonai*) in suffering, redemptive love. Later theology will stress that the Spirit personifies the mutual self-giving love of Father and Son. The Spirit is the spirit of the crucified, risen Christ. The cross of Jesus, therefore, discloses neither a unitarian nor binitarian God. Through and through, the cross and exaltation remain an event of Father, Son and Holy Spirit.

The Gospels highlight Jesus' awareness of his Father's closeness to him. They also evidence his consciousness of his own empowerment through the Spirit of God. In his ministry, Jesus experiences God both as Abba (father) and as Spirit.[27] For the Johannine tradition, however, it was on the cross that the Holy Spirit was newly poured forth upon creation. For this same tradition the blessed Spirit is both poured upon all creation and draws all creation unto God. The Spirit exists to unite—the love of Father and Son is bodied forth in all its unity by the Holy Spirit. This Spirit *is* the spirit of Christ—'the Lord is the Spirit and the Spirit is the Lord' (2 Cor. 3:17). Throughout the New Testament there is a tensive identity of Jesus and Spirit. This is an identity in difference: their unity is emphasised, yet both Son and Paraclete receive separate personal references. One can without exaggeration say that the self-giving of both Father and Son—referred to by the verb *paradidonai*—is the Spirit, distinct from both yet fully God.

For the Pauline writings, the power of the Spirit is an all pervasive reality. The Spirit is the spirit of Jesus' resurrection and the guarantee of our own. The Spirit empowers the community's life as the community of the Lord. The same Spirit enables individual Christians in their service of each other. Finally, in the continuing work of the new creation the Holy Spirit is the motive force present even to inanimate creation as it, too, aspires to integral full redemption in the Son of God (Rom. 8:28).

The Old Testament adumbration of *Shekinah* takes on fresh shape here. The tensive identity, the difference in unity of Father, Son and blessed Spirit is affirmed in the newness of primitive Christianity. God is one. There is none other than the God of Exodus, of Covenant, of creation and recreation, of new Covenant. In fashioning the new creation God's presence disclose not a multiplicity but an undreamed-of richness. It is the richness of the loving creativity of the Father, the sacrificial, self-emptying of the Son and the faithful enablement of the Holy Spirit. This presence (*Shekinah*) dwells not in temple or church but—in the first place—in the persons of all who serve God in sincerity and truth.

The trinitarian understanding of God's presence is, therefore, economical. It arises, that is to say, from the experience of the history of God's solidarity with a suffering world which through Christ has been given new hope. Focused on the life work of Jesus, that hope is indebted for vitality and perdurance to the Spirit of God. This spirit enables Christians to address God as Abba (Rom. 8:15; Gal. 4:6) and to confess that Jesus is Lord (Rom. 8:26). From the same Spirit comes the empowerment of the Church in ministry, eucharist and service.

The history of God's solidarity with suffering pushes us beyond the dilemma of theism and atheism. Theism and atheism are mirror images. Working upon each other incessantly they present God as a monarchic figure who must either be submissively obeyed or angrily rejected. Their common subject is Isaac Newton's 'master of the universe'. As against this, a trinitarian understanding discloses the compassion of God even to suffering and death. It expresses God's sympathetic accompaniment of both creation and new creation through the enabling presence of the Holy Spirit. It is respectful both of the transcendence of God and the involvement of God in a broken world. This understanding of God transcends pantheism (with its confusion of God and cosmos), and deism (with its relegation of God to the sidelines of world history).

The thrust of Christian faith is from creation to new creation. New creation is effected not by effortless word but through suffering. Only in the crucified and risen Christ have all things been made new. And yet, old sinful ways, patterns and structures remain: there is much yet to do in filling up the suffering of Christ. New creation is subject to the tension of the 'already' and the 'not yet'. On the one hand, we can say that all has been achieved through Chirst and his Spirit in the gift of God. On the other hand, we have to say that all remains yet to do. In late twentieth-century society—indeed in Ireland of this time—the brokenness of creation is evident. At the personal, societal and ecological levels the threat to the integrity of creation is manifest. The assault on the environment, the dominance of unjust and cruel structures, the refractoriness of human freedom disqualify facile optimism. At times, the cross of Christ seems to have been carried in vain. In the midst of this, Christian faith must surely speak a word of trinitarian hope. It must proclaim God's passion for life. It must affirm God's presence in pain and defeat as well as in joy and attainment. It must hold to a hope for the eschatological future. The warrant for such hope remains the trinitarian history of God's involvement with the suffering world. It is only as we hold to a presence of God's enabling spirit that such a hope can endure and be effective.

We are forced back to the gospel's perception that God is love. God is love—suffering, patient, steadfast love. We have come to know this love in Christ through his Spirit. Here, theological search halts and is made to consider the demands of God's love. God's love, in its solidarity with the sufferer, challenges us to be and to do in like manner'. god's love is trinitarian and it is practical: 'If you want to know what the trinity looks like be filled with the Holy Spirit and look at the cross.'[28] Loving God is not a simple matter of affective knowledge. As disclosed in Jesus, it is self-giving and sacrificial. It is *kenosis* or self-emptying. The cross of Christ shows that the greatest power is in the extreme of weakness. From the cross, on Easter day, emerges the triumph of suffering love. Here indeed is the hope of the hopeless. Here also is a disclosure of *how* God is. God is not the monarch before whom no-one can stand. Rather, God is the one whose suffering love reconciles creation in its brokenness and enables divided people to become sisters and brothers. People can stand before God in autonomy. We are allowed to be dialogue partners with God.

Christian experience discloses the process of God's love in the history of Jesus. This history is a sacrament of the Trinity. God is not petrified in majestic solitude or boring immobility. God is not the unmoved mover of Aristotle, with all the attendant connotations of inertia. In the triune God resides the dynamic love which early Christianity experienced at Easter and Pentecost. Easter and Pentecost disclose an event 'containing within it all the modalities of love which . . . appear in created forms in the course of the world's relationship with God'.[29]

We can dare to speak of a divine mutability. God changes, not as a response to manipulation, but because of the vitality of trinitarian life. Here is the give and take of overbrimming love. The law of divine life is to love. To love requires giving and receiving. To love spells dynamism and vitality. All these can be affirmed of God. The ancient terminology of *perichoresis* (Greek) and *circuminsessio* (Latin) implies this unity of life and love. The persons of the Trinity share a community of life; it brooks neither separation nor division. Such community of life is self-renewing and yet never-altering. Perhaps the patristic image of a fountain of living water is helpful. Ever renewed, ever the same, the fountain is at once self-defined and other-refreshing. In the Christian conception, the Trinity is the beauty 'ever-ancient, ever-new', which neither changes with the ages nor ceases to be the fount of life and love.

To revert to the question 'Can God change?' one must answer at once No and Yes. With the thrust of tradition we must say No, if change means imperfection, deficiency or impotence. With the thrust of tradition we must say Yes, if change means the give and take of love, the solidarity of concern, the attentiveness of care. The coherence of these two answers—Yes and No—is part of the Christian sense of who and how God is. Can God suffer, it is asked. Again we have to say both No and Yes. God cannot suffer a physical hurt. We cannot predicate suffering of God in a univocal sense. In this sense, one must say God cannot suffer. Nevertheless, one cannot ignore the scriptural references to the *com-passio* of God. God took the form of a servant, even to death on a cross. The Father 'gave up'—and therefore suffered—the death of his beloved Son. The Son of God entered our flesh, carried our cross and died our death. Here are both 'giving up' and self-emptying (*kenosis*). Throughout the laborious process of the new creation there is a *kenosis* of the Spirit who accompanies the new creation in power and is yet patient of its long struggle carried out in hardship, disappointment and tears. Neither creation as a whole nor humanity as part of it, are deprived of God's involvement for an instant. Nor are suffering and failure an evidence of God's inability or lack of concern. One might invert the argument: God's trinitarian involvement with our world takes the form of self-giving, suffering love. That involvement is disclosed in the laborious task of drawing the new creation from the old, the 'new man' from the 'old man'. With Herbert McCabe we can say *not* that 'God eternally suffers' but that 'the eternal power of God is love; and this as expressed in history must be suffering'.[30]

At this point theology must have regard to its limitations. The language of Yes and No is not the language of ambiguity or equivocation. Rather it articulates respect at once for the hiddenness of mystery and for the disclosure of mystery. It is surely paradoxical to say that God can change with the mutability of love while proclaiming God's constancy which transcends flux of any kind. It is paradoxical to say that God can suffer while proclaiming that God is transcendent to every influence from outside Godself. The theologian who attempts to hold these affirmations together is driven towards the concept of analogy. Analogy is a flexible instrument which rises above both ambiguity (equivocation) and premature certainty (univocation). It permits us to make affirmations even about the inner Trinity while realising all the while that

170

these affirmations fall short of their mark. Analogical statements about God operate in that border area between the limits of human knowledge and the disclosure of mystery which is in the gift only of God.

If the approach of analogy is sensitively followed, on the ground of the privileged self-mediation of God in Jesus Christ—then we can made claims, diffidently yet confidently, even about the inner mystery of God's trinity. We can attribute change and even suffering to God without crossing over into fable, legend and superstition. Still more, we can affirm that our mottled history with its negative and its positive, its sorrow and its joy, its despair and its hope are somehow taken up into the life and love of the triune God. One may perhaps speak once again of panentheism. Our world, our history, our personal being retain their creaturely autonomy. Yet they subsist in the presence of God who takes into the trinitarian life the minutest detail of the world's trauma. The task of re-creation is, therefore, to be related to the work of Trinity in creation, redemption and integral salvation or sanctification.

A pilgrim's theology must keep the aspirations and griefs of its time and place centrally in mind. In doing so it requires some stand-point, perspective or interpretative stance. A theology of God must be free, creative and flexible. Such freedom, creativity and flexibility are shown in the best of theology's own history. However, a Christian theology of God cannot ignore certain milestones for its pilgrimage. One such milestone signals the life-affirming disposition of God from whom comes all life, all joy, all gladness. God is the God of life and flourishing rather than of death and decay. Another guideline for a pilgrim's theology is that God goes with all who suffer. God is the God of solidarity with the victim. God is partisan in solidarity with the oppressed. Finally, a third and irreplaceable guideline is that richness of God we call Trinity. For Christian theology, certainly for a pilgrim's theology, it is necessary to root all its affirmations in the real world of nuclear threat, of massive armament, of hunger and disease, of horrendous suffering. Theology must also keep in mind the involvement of God with our history not just as monarchic deity but as tri-unity in unity. Such involvement is in hiddenness, suffering and death. It is also in joy, empowerment, and sisterhood/brotherhood. It promises the vindication of the fallen in the glorious triumph of resurrection and the hope of a renewed creation.

Neither milestones nor guidelines are a brake on movement. There is good reason to seek new ways of expressing the mystery of God. One can indeed speak of God as friend (McFague), as fellow traveller (A. N. Whitehead), as motherly father (Moltmann), as ground and stay of being (Paul Tillich). By these and other models, contemporary theology seeks to mitigate the stern transcendence of earlier times. For people who have experienced the loneliness of modern life and who cherish nature and personhood as revelatory, the immanence of God evokes an enthusiastic response. Having learned something from Freud, we are wary of starkly personal images of transcendence. Having learned something from Marx, we are critical of the use made of the image of the 'Great King on his mighty throne'. Nevertheless, if Christian theology is to remain true to itself it must retain the distinction between God and God's world. Likewise, it must be clear that the perfection we call personality is in God to the highest degree. Theology will be at its best when, starting with the tri-unity of God, it moves on to an emphasis on God's oneness, God's otherness and God's involvement with creation as Father, Son and blessed Spirit. Thus it will avoid casting God as one individual over and against others. *That* would limit both God and creatures. It would incur all the old criticisms about subjection of people to a despot, albeit benign. The three persons who are the divine unity cannot be depicted in this static, monarchic way. The trinitarian life of God is an eventful richness, transcending the limitations of all our ideas of personhood. Its privileged manifestation is in the sacrificial love of Jesus directed towards the Father as well as in the continuing hope given in the power of God's Holy Spirit.

For Christian theology the triune God must be confessed: 'we believe in Father, Son and Spirit' Like all doctrines, the trinitarian confession must be allowed to point beyond itself into something greater than the words in which it is framed. Like all religious language, it is a symbol—with the full power and full truth-content of symbol at its best. The eventful,

172

tripersonal action of the one God in creation, incarnation and recreation confronts us with a God who sunders all the constrictions which limit our understanding. Hence, the confession of the Trinity is not exclusive of other attempts to formulate the mystery of God. And yet, it must remain paradigmatic for all Christian reflection on God.

The tripersonal action of God shatters the awful dualisms which beset the history of human existence: dualism in sexual, racial and class terms. God, the triune God, pushes us to dismantle these and encourages us in doing so. A pilgrim's theology enters upon the work of overcoming sexism, racism and all other forms of domination. Must it not also insist that the God of pilgrims rejects these dualisms and does so precisely as *this* Father, *this* Son and *this* Spirit. Without prejudice to the fight against sexism in liturgy, theology and practice we must surely say that Father, Son and Spirit remain normative for theological reflection and confession. Neither male chauvinism nor extreme feminism must be allowed to hi-jack or discredit the trinitarian model. The Trinity, as confession, points to the richness of God's life and love, not exhaustively, not exclusively, but in a way privileged by its centrality to Christian history. One does not root out sexist bias by suppressing Father, Son and Spirit to replace these by Mother, Sister and Friend. Nor is it a matter of numerical balance in the use of male and female pronouns. It *is* a matter of reading aright the signal of God's wonderful action in our history even today, where:

—the fatherliness of the Father is the gift of life and flourishing, the 'letting be' that human parents try to attain and frequently do not;
—the *motherliness* of the Father is the attentive and frequently silent concern that mothers so beautifully show;
—the sonship of the Son is love even unto death on the cross so that sisterhood/brotherhood may once again be held out as the aim of human relationship;
—the *brotherhood* of the son is a solidarity with those who suffer and a promise that their vindication has its first fruit in the resurrection of Easter;
—the *comfort* of the Spirit is empowerment to build a

Church and a world in which there is 'neither male nor female, neither Jew nor Gentile, neither slave nor free' (Gal. 3:28).

Appendix

Knowledge of God is the Practice of Justice

The Old Testament affirmation is very clear. To know God is to do justice. This is an identity rather than a consequence. One does not first know and then do. Much less does one do justice and then know God. To do justice *is* to know God. The knowledge of God is practical. It is an act of trust, commitment and acknowledgment. It is never pure theory. For the main thrust of the Old Testament, to know God is an active, vital thing. It is recognition of God as person with a corresponding pattern of activity. The knowledge of God is bound up with the practice of justice. This emphasis on practice is surely one of the things specific to Hebrew and Judaic faith. Right knowing is linked to right doing. Ignorance or not-knowing is not inadvertence but rather not-noticing, rejecting or even revolt.

For the Old Testament the denial of justice means that God is not really known even where the name of Yahweh is studiously invoked. Honour with the lips only is an empty formula. It touches, not on God, but on a void. Injustice leads to an inability even to invoke the name of God. Those who do injustice erect idols. They say 'to a tree—"You are my father," and to a stone—"You gave me birth"'.[1] Only when it is too late will the name of God be invoked: 'Have you not *just now* called to me,—my father you are the friend of my youth.' Here lies the subversive quality of the Old Testament. In the name of God it rejects injustice and the distortion spawned by injustice. Where the widow is spurned, God is insulted. Where the orphan is overlooked God is neglected. Where the stranger is ill-treated God is degraded. This surely is the meaning of the text of Proverbs—he who mocks the poor insults his maker (Prov. 17:5). With the loss of reverence for the poor, the knowledge of God is also lost. Notice the instructions given to

175

the chosen people as they stand at the entrance to the promised land. They are to remember that the land is pure gift. It is neither a prize nor an achievement. Rather is it a responsibility. The Hebrews are to keep in mind that once they were in slavery and were liberated by God's initiative. This dangerous memory challenges any subsequent institution of slavery or oppression. The challenge is in the name of God who liberated the Hebrews to make them free men and women.

Israel did repress its subversive memory. It did so especially under the kings. Yet, it is clear that the prophetic strain did not allow the memory to become totally erased. That memory arose with power in Amos and in Isaiah. Deutero-Isaiah identifies the service of God with the service of righteousness and justice in very secular things: 'Is not this the kind of fasting I want: Remove the chains of oppression and the yoke of injustice and let the oppressed go free. Share your food with the hungry and open your homes to the homeless poor. Give clothes to those who have nothing to wear' (Isaiah 58:6-7). Proto-Isaiah has the same injunction:

> Wash yourselves clean. Stop all this evil...
> ...and learn to do right. See that justice is done...
> help those who are oppressed
> give orphans their rights
> and defend widows (Is. 1:16-18)

A dominant perception of Judaism is that God responds most clearly, quickly and favourably to the needs of the poor. The prophets consistently reiterate that God favours the poor and is known in their midst. Rabbi David Rosen reminds us that the defence of the poor is where God is 'seen' to particular effect. King David calls on God five times to 'scatter his enemies'. Yet it is only in response to the cry of the poor that God answers thus:

> For the oppression of the poor and the cry of the needy, then I will arise says the Lord.[2]

More than in cult or psalm God is found in the cause of the poor. Knowledge of God is practical. It lies in right doing. To use our current jargon, orthopraxis feeds orthodoxy. It can be argued that Judaism kept alive the tension between priest and king, on the one hand, and prophet, on the other. Here, one cannot make an absolute contradiction. There were kings who heeded the imperative to justice. There were court-prophets who prostituted the prophetic word. Nevertheless, as Walter Brueggemann points out: 'It is the business of the prophets to discern what kings cannot see and to articulate what kings cannot bear. Their spectrum of expectation and their rigour in honesty are beyond royal possibilities. So they think unthinkable thoughts and speak unspeakable words which kings can never tolerate or bear to face.'[3]

II

Matthew 25. The Parable of the Last Judgment

Attend for a moment, not primarily to the judgment, but to the recognition of Jesus, and thus of God. Who are the 'nations'? Who are the hungry, thirsty, sick? How does one know Christ, and therefore, God, in the 'least of the brethren'? Exegetes have argued widely and long about what to the ordinary reader might appear open and simple. Some scholars limit 'the least of the breathren' to Christians, and those being judged to non-Christians. Others see here a standard of judgment for all Christians on who they have treated their fellow-Christians. Who does not recognise the needy sister/brother in her/his need, does not recognise Christ. Finally, yet others argue that Matthew 25 is about the judgment of all people without exception on how they have treated their sister/brother who was literally hungry, thirsty, imprisoned. It is the last of these possibilities which is adopted here.

The criterion by which people are judged is neither cult nor mysticism. It is rather the doing of the fraternal/sororal thing. On this hinges whether one has recognised Christ and hence God. The recognition of Christ is tied into solidarity with the 'little ones'. In the Christian context, we can say by extension that to enter the need of the suffering other is to recognise God.

III

Luke 4. The Sermon in the Synagogue

With Luke 4 we encounter the descriptive *leitmotif* of Jesus' ministry. The text sums up all he tried to do. It reaches into the tradition from which he emerged.[4] With the text we are in the middle of the Jesus-tradition on the kingdom of God. The kingdom is announced, inaugurated,, 'this day in your hearing'. It is not 'up there' or 'later on'. For Jesus of Nazareth it is related to the healing of the blind, the deaf, the lame and the poor. The practice of this kingdom entails a new and different vision of God. It changes prevailing assumptions as to where God is to be found. The temple is not the temple of human construction of vestments, incense and precious stones, of priests and hierarchs. God *may* be here but not necessarily, and certainly not predictably. The *templum Dei*, the place of God's glory, is the people of God, the suffering, the excluded, the despised. Here is where God is known. *Here* is where God's glory dwells.

IV

The Magnificat (Luke 1: 46-55)

The deposition of the mighty from their thrones and the exaltation of the lowly is surely a subversive proposal. So too is the filling of the hungry and the dismissal of the rich from their situation of privilege. This God is a revolutionary God, a subversive God, a God who takes sides. Taken literally, the Magnificat asserts that God is on the side of those who search for justice and against those who deprive people of life and flourishing. A reference much used in the writings of Gustavo Gutiérrez is that 'the God of the masters is not the same'. What can this statement mean? It reminds us that masters of every kind create their own God. Confident in their power they construct a private God to whom they give some of the biblical traits. José Comblin argues that the God of the army, the land owner, the oligarchy, is alive and well. Many are the reassurances that the God of power, money and status is both

178

courted and worshipped. Characteristics of traditional theology are willingly accorded this God—power, rule, anger, unpredictability, readiness to punish, justice of a strictly judgmental kind. This God is made to underwrite stability, compliance, obedience and resignation.

There is one trait which the God of the masters does not possess. The God of the powerful is never the God of justice or of social change. The God who loves mercy and not sacrifice is not the God of the powerful. The God who 'fills the hungry and sends the rich empty away' is not the God of the oligarchs. The God who does justice to the poor is not the God of unbridled gain. For that reason, in the absence of a thorough-going conversion, those who worship the God of the masters cannot know the God of the Bible.

This is a radical claim with radical implications. It affirms that ideologies lie at the heart even of Christianity. Vested interests try to harness God to their own purposes. They attempt to rationalise their own interests in theological terms. The true God is not harnessed to any chariot. The question arises as to whether the same God is worshipped by the exploiter and the exploited. Can the oppresser and the oppressed share the same eucharist? If deeds bespeak faith, surely the vast difference in patterns of action shows forth a greater difference in faith than of confessional divides. All too frequently liturgy has slipped over these differences. Where they have been made explicit, it is to exclude those taken to be subversive of the established order. 'Denied the sacraments', they were left in no doubt that the institutional Church had little place for them. In the meantime, what of the 'captains and the kings'? What of the militarists of all hues whose only legitimacy might be a chest full of medals and decorations? What of the architects of unjust economic programmes which have driven many people to the wall not just in third world countries but far nearer home?

If an ambiguity lies over the common worship or common theology of exploiter and exploited, the ambiguity resides not in God but in the ideological manipulation of the things of faith. Hence, it is a theological task to exercise a critique of all theological language for its use of alienating ideology. This critical task is also a *self*-critical task. It calls for an explication of one's own bias, stance or option. Theology must attend in a particular way to the strong emphasis on justice and care for the needy contained in its own privileged sources, especially the Scriptures. We are led to affirm that while God is indeed the God of all people, nevertheless God addresses us all through the call of the poor and needy. God speaks to us in their voice. Whatever contradicts the call for justice is from a source other than the God of the Bible, the God of Jesus Christ. Archbishop Oscar Romero used to emphasise that God exludes no-one from love and mercy. Yet, according to the martyred archbishop, the offer of love and mercy comes through the cause of the wretched of the earth. It comes through the need of the little ones. Therefore, the God of the masters is not the same as the God of the poor. One is an idol. The other is the God of the Bible. This God addresses *all* but from a definite stand-point. This God is to be found in the midst of the work of justice but is missing from the work of injustice.

V

The Messianic Vision of God

A major element of all prophetic writing is protest against the denial of justice. It is as if to say that where justice is denied there God is banished. The prophet Amos laments:

> They sell the righteous for silver and the needy
> for a pair of shoes.
> They trample the head of the poor into the dust
> and turn aside the way of the afflicted (Amos 2:6-7)

The prophet is reacting to unjust suffering and saying that it should not be so. The biblical response to unmerited suffering does not halt at pure denunciation. Its vision is a messianic vision. It looks to an intervention by God against unrighteousness and injustice (the day of the Lord) and to a new, better order which would correspond fully to the will of God. There is a utopian vision in Judaism—in particular, in the prophets. Theirs is a hope for the Messiah of justice who will institute a kingdom of right order (*misphat*), of justice (*tzedek*,

180

tzedikah), of peace (*shalom*). They look to a world free of domination. Their vision is expressed variously but always symbolically. What more powerful alternative vision is there than that described at Isaiah 9:2-7:

> The people who walked in darkness have seen a great light. They lived in a land of shadows but now light is shining on them. You have given them great joy, Lord, you have made them happy. For you have broken the yoke that burdened them and the rod that beat their shoulders...
>
> A child is born to us, a son is given to us, and he will be our ruler.
>
> He will be called 'Wonderful Counsellor', 'Mighty God', 'Eternal Father', 'Prince of Peace'.
>
> His kingdom will always be at peace.

Franz Mussner remarks that 'Such visions are in the blood of Judaism.'[5] Like every utopian vision the messianic dream has both cost and benefit. Its cost is that it can generate a melancholia of waiting—'a life of deferment where nothing can be done definitely, nothing can be irrevocably established'.[6] Or else it can generate one of the many kinds of fanatical outbursts which, overestimating its own strength, leads to bitter disappointment and draws down savage repression. Yet, we stand greatly indebted to Judaic messianism. It keeps open the idea of God's future. That is to say, a future of justice, love and peace wherein the vindication of the sufferer, the excluded and the victim will be manifest. A future of this kind is no more than an illusion if two truths are not affirmed. The first is the victory over death. The second is the necessity to work here and now for anticipations of God's kingdom.

Short Bibliography

Ballantine, Samuel E., *The Hidden God*, Oxford University Press, 1983.

Congar, Yves, *Mysterium Templi*, Westminster: Newman Press, 1962.

Congar, Yves, *The Revelation of God*, London and New York: Darton, Longman and Todd, 1968.

Davies, Brian, *Thinking about God*, London: Chapman, 1985.

Edwards, Denis, *Human Experience of God*, New York: Paulist, 1983.

Fennell, Desmond, *Irish Catholics Since 1916*, Dublin: Dominican Publications, 1984.

Ford, Adam, *Universe: God, Man and Science,* London: Hodder and Stoughton, 1986.

Forristal, Desmond, *The Mystery of God*, Dublin: Veritas, 1980.

Frossard, André, *God Exists. I have Met Him,* London: Collins, 1970.

Gallagher, M. P., *Help My Unbelief*, Dublin: Veritas, 1986.

Hastings, Adrian, *The Faces of God*, London: Chapman, 1975

Harrison, Jim, *The Darkness of God. Theology After Hiroshima*, London: SCM, 1982.

Haught, John, *What is God?* Dublin: Gill and MacMillan, 1986.

Jung, C.G., *Answer to Job*, London: Ark, 1984.

Kearney, Richard, *Poétique du Possible*, Paris: Beauchesne, 1984.

Kasper, Walter, *Jesus the Christ*, London: Burns and Oates/New York: Paulist, 1970.

Kasper, Walter; *The God of Jesus Christ*, London: SCM, 1983.

Knight, George, *I AM. This is my Name,* Grand Rapids: Eerdmanns, 1983.

Küng, Hans, *Does God Exist?*, London: Collins, 1978.

Lane, D.A., *The Experience of God*, New York: Paulist, 1981.

Levinas, Emmanuel, *Totality and Infinity*, Pittsburgh: Duquesnse University Press/The Hague: Nijhoff, 1969.

Lubac, Henri De, *Sur Les Chemins de Dieu,* Aubier: Foi Vivante, 1966.

McCabe, Herbert, *God Matters*, London: Chapman, 1987.

McDonagh, Enda, *Between Chaos and New Creation*, Dublin: Gill and MacMillan, 1986.

McFague, Sallie, *Models of God. Theology for an Ecological, Nuclear Age*, London: SCM, 1987.

Mackey, James P., *Modern Theology—A Sence of Direction*, Oxford University Press, 1987.

Mackey, *The Christian Experience of God as Trinity*, London: SCM, 1983.

Macquarrie, John, *In Search of Deity*, London: SCM, 1984.

Mangan, Celine, *Can We Still Call God Father*, Dublin: Dominican Publications, 1984.

Mascall, Eric, *Existence and Analogy*, London: Darton, Longman and Todd, 1966.

Masterson, Patrick, *Atheism and Alienation*, Dublin: Gill and MacMillan, 1971.

Moltmann, Jürgen, *The Theology of Hope*, London: SCM, 1967.

Moltmann, Jürgen, *The Crucified God*, London: SCM, 1974.

Moltmann, Jürgen, *The Trinity and the Kingdom of God*, London: SCM, 1981.

Murray, John Courtney, *The Problem of God*, Yale, 1964.

O'Murchu, Diarmuid, *The God Who Becomes Redundant*, Dublin: Mercier/London: Fowler Wright, 1986.

Rahner, Karl, *Foundations of Christian Theology*, New York: Seabury, 1978.

Reuther, Rosemary Radford, *Sexism and God Talk*, London: SCM, 1983.

Robinson, J. A. T., *Honest to God*, London: SCM, 1963.

Robinson, J. A. T., *Exploration into God*, London: SCM, 1967.

Robinson, J. A. T., *In the End God*, London: Collins (Fontana), 1968.

Schillebeeckx, Edward, *God the Future of Man*, London-Sydney, Sheed and Ward, 1969.

Schillebeeckx, Edward, *Jesus. An Experiment in Christology*, London: Collins, 1979.

Schillebeeckx, Edward, *Christ: The Christian Experience in the Modern World*, London: SCM, 1980.

Segundo, J. L., *Our Idea of God*, New York: Maryknoll, 1974.

Shea, John, *Stories of God*, Chicago: The Thomas More Press, 1978.

Song, Choan-Seng, *The Compassionate God. An Exercise in the Theology of Transposition*, London: SCM, 1982.

Stannard, Russell, *Science and the Renewal of Belief*, London, SCM, 1982.

Surin, Kenneth, *Theology and the Problem of Evil*, Oxford: Basil Blackwell, 1986.

Terrien, Samuel, *The Elusive Presence*, New York: Harper and Row, 1983.

Tillich, Paul, *The Courage to Be*, London: Collins (Fontana), 1962.
Trible, Phyllis, *God and the Rhetoric of Sexuality*, Philadelphia: Fortress Press, 1978.

Useful Articles
Daly, Gabriel, "Knowing God", *The Furrow*, July, 1979, 436-49.
O'Hanlon, Gerard, "Does God Change", *Irish Theological Quarterly* 3, (1987), 161-83.

Notes

Chapter 1. No Easy Certitude, pp. 2-19.

1. M. P. Gallagher, *Help My Unbelief*, Dublin: Veritas 1986, 17.
2. See his *Aenigma Fidei*, *P.L.*, 180, 390 c, 'Sed in hac quaestione Deum videndi plus nobis videtur valere vivendi modum quam loquendi'.
3. Gabriel Daly, 'Knowing God', *The Furrow* July 1979, 447.
4. M. P. Gallagher, op. cit., 123.
5. Ludwig Wittgenstein, *Tractatus Logico-Philosophicus*, London: Routledge and Kegan Paul, 1922, preface.
6. Edward Schillebeeckx, *Christ: The Christian Experience in the Modern World*, London: SCM, 1980, 808.
7. Ibid.
8. Thus Frossard's title: *God Exists. I have Met Him.* London: Collins, 1970.
9. Cited in Gallagher, op. cit., 63.
10. See note 3.
11. E. Schillebeeckx, op. cit., 808.
12. Adrian Hastings, *The Faces of God*, London Chapman, 1975, 3.
13. J. L. Segundo, *Our Idea of God*, New York: Orbis, 1974, 8.
14. Choan-Seng Song, *The Compassionate God. An Exercise in the Theology of Transposition*, London: SCM, 1982, 2.
15. Cited in G. Daly, 'Knowing God' in *The Furrow*, July 1979, 443.
16. J. L. Segundo, op. cit., 79.
17. Gregory Baum, *The Social Imperative*, New York-Ramsey-Toronto: Paulist, 1979, 47.
18. C. G. Jung, *Answer to Job*, London: Ark, 1984, 94.
19. Hugo Meynell, *Grace versus Nature*, London-Melbourne: Sheed and Ward, 1965, 90.
20. *Gaudium et Spes* (Pastoral Constitution on The Church in the modern World), art. 19.
21. John Macquarrie, *In Search of Deity*, London: SCM, 1984, 49.
22. Cited by Jürgen Moltmann, *The Crucified God*, London: SCM, 1974, 220.
23. F. Dostoyevsky, *The Brothers Karamazov*, (trans. D. Magarshack), London: Harmondsworth, 1958, 274-87.
24. See J. Moltmann, op cit., 219 et seq.
25. Paul Tillich, *The Courage to Be*, London: Collins (Fontana), 1962, 179. The 'emergent humanism of liberty' is examined skilfully by Patrick Masterson, *Atheism and Alienation*, Dublin: Gill and Macmillan, 1971.
26. J. L. Segundo, op. cit., 36.
27. *Ecclesiam Suam*, encyclical letter of Paul VI, para. 104.

185

28. T. S. Eliot, cited by Desmond Forristal in *The Mystery of God*, Dublin: Veritas, 1980, 63.
29. See the stimulating article of André Dumas, 'The New Attraction of Neo-Paganism' in *Concilium*, 177 (I/1985), ed. Claude Geffré and J. P. Jossua, 81-9. Citation at 81.
30. Ibid., 81.
31. 'Monotheismus als politisches Problem (1935)' in *Theologische Traktate*, 45-148.
32. David Nicholls, 'Images of God and the State: Political Analogy and Religious Discourse', in *Theological Studies* 42 (1981), 195-215.
33. José Comblin, *Frontiers of Theology in Latin America*, London: SCM, 1980, 61.
34. Leonardo Boff, *Church, Charism and Power*, London: SCM, 1985, 113.
35. For a good treatment of the theology of God from the standpoint of process theology see Norman Pittenger, *Picturing God*, London: SCM, 1982.
36. Andrew Greeley, *Unsecular Man. The Persistence of Religion*, New York: Schocken, 1972, 151-70.
37. C. G. Jung in *The Secret of the Golden Fleece*, Éranos Jahrbuch, 1946, vol. VIII, 400.
38. Karl Rahner, *Foundations of Christian Faith*, New York: Seabury, 1978, 57.
39. Ibid., 49.
40. Victor White, *God and the Unconscious*, London: Fontana, 1952, 28; J. A. T. Robinson, *In the End God*, London: Fontana, 1968, 12.

Chapter 2. By My Deeds Shall You Know Me, pp. 20-36.
1. Van A. Harvey, *The Historian and the Believer*, London: SCM, 1967, 257.
2. G. Von Rad, *Old Testament Theology*, vol. I, 138.
3. E. Schillebeeckx, *Christ*, 522.
4. John Shea, *Stories of God*, Chicago: The Thomas More Press, 1978, 101.
5. Ibid., 102 and 107.
6. *Qu'est-ce que Dieu. Hommage à l'abbé Daniel Coppieters de Gibson*, Brussels: Publications des Facultés St. Louis, 1985, 547.
7. See the article 'God' by John W. Wright S.J. in *The New Dictionary of Theology*, ed. J. A. Komonchak, Mary Collins and D. A. Lane, Dublin: Gill and Macmillan, 1987, 423–36.
8. Martin Buber, *The Prophetic Faith*, New York: Harper and Row, 1960, 37.
9. The text runs: 'Any Israelite or any foreigner living in Israel who curses the Lord shall be stoned.'
10. Karl Barth, *Church Dogmatics*, I, I, Edinburgh: T. and T. Clark, 1963, 369-70.
11. E. Bloch, *Das Prinzip Hoffnung*, Frankfort, 1967, vol. III, 1457-8.
12. John Courtney Murray, *The Problem of God*, Yale, 1964, 10.
13. Yves Congar, *The Revelation of God*, London: Darton, Longman and Todd/New York: Herder and Herder, 1968, 88.

14. J. A. T. Robinson, *Honest to God*, London: SCM, 1963, 36 et seq.
15. G. Gutiérrez, *A Theology of Liberation*, New York: Orbis, 1973, 159.
16. Y. Congar, *Mysterium Templi*, Westminster: Newman Press, 1962, 15.
17. Cited in J. Moltmann, 'The Inviting Unity of the Triune God' in *Concilium*, 177 (I/1985), 53.
18. Ex. 14: 11-12.
19. E. McDonagh, *Between Chaos and New Creation*, Dublin: Gill and MacMillan, 109.
20. Ibid., 110.

Chapter 3. The God of Mercy, Justice and Compassion, pp. 37-54.

1. Gen. 31:19.
2. I Sam. 26:19.
3. Micah 4:5.
4. Deut. 4:35.
5. Bernhard Lang, 'No God but Jahweh', *Concilium* 177 (I/1985), 45.
6. Exod. 3:7-10.
7. Yves Congar, *The Revelation of God*, 49.
8. E. Schillebeeckx, *Christ*, 95.
9. Blaise Pascal, *Pensées*, (trans. A. J. Krailscheimer), Penguin: Harmondsworth, 1966, 586.
10. See Samuel E. Balentine, *The Hidden God*, Oxford University Press, 1983, 172.
11. Ibid., 125.
12. Ibid., 173.
13. Samuel Terrien, *The Elusive Presence*, New York: Harper and Row, 1983.
14. Adrian Hastings, *The Faces of God*, London: Chapman, 1975, 4.
15. Cf. Buber's fascinating treatment in *On Zion*, 114.
16. Jurgen Moltmann, *The Theology of Hope*, London: SCM, 1967, 99.
17. S. Terrien, op. cit., 63 et seq.; 106 et seq.
18. Jürgen Moltmann, *The Theology of Hope*, 97.
19. Ibid., 105.

Chapter 4: The Humanity of God, pp. 55-71.

1. Racine, *Athalie*, Act II, Scene V.
2. John 1:18.
3. Cf. George Knight's impressive chapter on Immanuel-Jehoshua in *I Am: This is My Name. The God of the Bible and the Religions of Man*, Grand Rapids, Michigan: Eerdmans, 1983, 49-59.
4. John Shea, *Stories of God*, 119.
5. Geo. Knight, op. cit., 72.
6. There is a vast literature here. In regard to living with a 'modicum of relativity' cf. James P. Mackey's evocative study *Modern Theology. A Sense of Direction*, O.U.P., 1987, esp. chapters 2, 3 and 4.
7. Ibid., 31.
8. A notable exception is Jesus' cry on the cross: 'My God, my God, why did you abandon me?' (Mark 15:34). The diverse strands of Abba

tradition are: Mark; material special to Matthew; material special to Luke: John; special *logia* material (Document Q).

9. Jeremiah 31:20—'Israel, you are my dearest son, the child I love best...'
Isaiah 63:16—'You are our father. Our ancestors Abraham and Jacob do not acknowledge us, but you Lord are our father, the one who has always rescued us.'
2 Samuel 7:14—'I will be his [Israel's] father and he will be my son.'
10. J. Jeremias tabulates Jesus' usage of Abba in the Gospels as follows: Mk (4 times); Luke (15 times); Matthew (42 times); John (109 times). Cf. Jeremias, 'Abba', *Studien zur neutestamentlichen Theologie and Zeitgeschichte*, Göttingen: Vandenhoeck and Ruprecht, 1966, 56; idem, 'Abba', *New Testament Theology*, vol. 1, London: SCM, 1971, 178 et seq.
11. Jeremias, *New Test. Theology*, 65.
12. Robert Hamerton-Kelly, *God the Father. Theology and Patriarchy in the Teaching of Jesus*, Philadelphia: Fortress 1979, 81.
13. Cf. Jeremias, 'Abba' in *Studien*, 164; also Hamerton-Kelly, *God the Father*, 73.
14. Jeremias, *New Test. Theology*, vol. 1, 98.
15. Celine Mangan, O.P., *Can We Still call God 'Father'*, Dublin: Dominican Publications, 1984, 55.
16. Mark 1:15.
17. Luke 11:20.
18. E. Schillebeeckx, *Jesus. An Experiment in Christology*, London: Collins, 1979, 146.
19. Luke 14:13.
20. Matt. 20:25-7.
21. Luke 4:21.
22. Leonardo Boff, *The Lord's Prayer*, New York: Orbis, 1983, 68.
23. E. Schillebeeckx, *Jesus*, 156.
24. Ibid., 157. The three exceptions are the parables of (i) the rich fool, (ii) Dives and Lazarus, (iii) the Pharisee and the publican.

Chapter 5. Justice before Stability, pp. 72-89.
1. E. Schillebeeckx, *Jesus*, 319.
2. Walter Kasper, *Jesus the Christ*, London: Burns and Oates/New York: Paulist, 1976, 116.
3. Luke 11:42; see also 12:56.
4. Edward Schillebeeckx, *God Among Us*, London: SCM, 1983, 75.
5. Mark 7:1-13; Matt. 15:1-9.
6. E. Schillebeeckx, *Jesus*, 301.
7. J. Moltmann, *The Crucified God*, 131.
8. See *Jesus*, 315.
9. Cited by J. Moltmann, *The Crucified God*, 136.
10. W. Kasper, op. cit., 114.
11. J. Ratzinger, *Introduction to Christianity*, London: Burns and Oates, 1969, 216.
12. Luke 24:21.
13. Acts 4:10; 2:22-4; 5:30; 10:40.

14. Gal. 1:4; Rom. 5:8; 8:32; Eph. 5:2; Mark 14:24 and 10:45; 1 Pet. 2:21-4.
15. 1 Cor. 15:3-5.
16. W. Kasper, *Jesus the Christ*, 145.
17. Brian Davies, *Thinking About God*, London: Chapman, 1985, 304. The words in parentheses are mine.
18. Albert Camus, *L'homme revolte*, Gallimard, 1951, 50 et seq. E.T. *The Rebel*, Hamish Hamilton, 1953.
19. Hans Küng, citing E. Bloch, *Das Prinzip Hoffnung*, in *Does God Exist?* London: Collins, 1980, 667.
20. Mark 15:38 = Matt. 27:51.
21. Chaon-Seng Song, *The Compassionate God*, 94.
22. Ibid., 96.
23. Gal. 3:28.
24. Choan-Seng Song, op. cit., 95.
25. Rosemary Radford Reuther, *Sexism and God-Talk*, London: SCM, 1983, 10-11.
26. E. Schillebeeckx, *God Among Us*, 74.

Chapter 6. Some Truths Revisited, pp. 90-110.
1. Rom. 1:18 et seq.; Acts 14:17; 17:28.
2. Cf. Claude Tresmantant's treatment of Luther's position in *Comment se pose aujourd'hui le problème de l'existence de Dieu*, Seuil, 1966, 435-6.
3. Karl Barth, *Church Dogmatics*, II, 1, 127.
4. Wis. 13:1-10.
5. Rom. 1:20.
6. Acts 17:27.
7. Rom. 1:23 and 25.
8. Karl Barth, op. cit., 123.
9. Dogmatic Constitution on the Catholic Faith (*Dei Filius*), esp. chapter on Revelation. See Denzinger 3021-6.
10. Latin American poet (unnamed) cited by J. L. Segundo, *Our Idea of God*, 181.
11. *Summa Theologiae*, Ia, IIae., q.2. art. 8.
12. Ibid.
13. Cf. Henri de Lubac's beautiful book *Sur Les Chemins de Dieu*, Aubier: Foi Vivante, 1966, esp. chapters 1 and 2; iden, *The Discovery of God*, London: Darton, Longman and Todd, 1960.
14. *Confessions*, Book 10, London-New York-Melbourne: the Scott Library, 247.
15. Ibid., 246.
16. Karl Rahner, 'Observations on the Doctrine of God', *Theological Investigations* vol. 9, London: Darton, Longman and Todd, 1972, 141.
17. The Anti-Modernist oath is to be distinguished from the pronouncement of the First Vatican Council and from Pius X's encyclical *Pascendi* (Sept. 1907). Required from all aspirants to major orders and to teaching posts its complete text is to be found at Denzinger 3538.
18. Hans Küng, *Does God Exist?*, 532.
19. André Frossard, *God Exists. I have met Him*, London: Collins, 1970.

20. See his preface to the 2nd edition of the *Critique of Pure Reason.*
21. Anthony Flew, *New Essays in Philosophical Theology*, London: SCM, 1966. 98-9.
22. See Küng, *Does God Exist?*, 540. The citation is from Kant's *Critique of Pure Reason.*
23. See John Courtney Murray, *The Problem of God*, 75.
24. Cf. John Macquarrie's excellent chapter 'The Theistic Proofs Reconsidered' in *In Search of Deity*, London: SCM, 1984, 199-211.
25. Hans Küng, *Does God Exist?* 550.
26. Karl Rahner, *Foundations*, 69.
27. Pope John Paul II, *Allocutio*, 10-7-85.
28. Cited by T.F. Torrance in *The Ground and Grammar of Theology*, Dublin-Belfast-Ottawa: Christian Journals, 1980, 5.
29. Pope John Paul II, *Allocutio*, 17-7-85.
30. Ibid.
31. Küng, *Does God Exist?*, 533 et seq.
32. See Pope John Paul II, *Allocutio*, 17-7-85.
33. Cited in Macquarrie, *In Search of Deity*, 211.
34. Wolfhart Pannenberg, *Basic Questions in Theology*, vol. II, London: SCM, 1971, 223.
35. 'God is known implicitly in every act of knowledge': St Thomas Aquinas and Duns Scotus share the principle. The meaning of the claim made in regard to the implicit knowledge of God is beautifully elaborated in de Lubac, *Sur les Chemins de Dieu*, 51.
36. Karl Rahner, 'Atheism and Implicit Christianity' in *Theological Investigations*, vol. 9, 154.
37. Raymond Pannikkar, *The Intra Religious Dialogue*, New York: Paulist, 1978, 57.
38. Desmond Fennell, *Irish Catholics since 1916*, Dublin: Dominican Publications, 1984, 25.
39. *Summa Theologiae*, IIa. IIae., q.1., art, 2, ad 2.
40. J. P. Mackey, *Modern Theology*, 128.
41. Citation from W. Pannenberg, *Basic Questions in Theology*, II, 238.
42. Cf. J. Habermas, *Knowledge and Human Interests*, London: Heinemann, 1972.
43. E. Schillebeeckx, *Jesus in Our Western Culture*, London: SCM, 1979, 80; The Synod of Barmen—*Theological Declaration of the Synod of the Confessing Church of Germany*, Barmen, 1934.
44. H. de Lubac, *The Discovery of God*, 6.
45. *Does God Exist?*, 575.

Chapter 7. The God of Life, Gladness, Daring, pp. 111-31.
1. I owe this consideration to J. G. Donders—cf. his *Creation and Human Dynamism, A Spirituality for Life*, Mystic, Connecticut: Twenty Third Publications, 1985.
2. *Creation and Human Dynamism*, 4.
3. *Why We Need a Third World Theology*, London: Ecumenical Association of Third World Theologians, CIIR, 1976, 13.

4. *Essai Philosophique sur les Probabilités*, Oeuvres Complètes VII, 1814, 6.
5. Adam Ford, *Universe: God, Man and Science*, London: Hodder and Stoughton, 1986, 60.
6. Rupert Sheldrake, *A New Science of Life*, London: Paladin Books, 1983.
7. A. Ford, op. cit., 11.
8. Peter Atkin, cited by Ford, op. cit., 69.
9. See Russell Stannard, *Science and the Renewal of Belief*, London: SCM, 1982, 101.
10. Karl Adam, 'Die Theologie der Krisis', *Hochland*, II (1926), 271-86.
11. A. N. Whitehead, *Process and Reality*, New York: The Free Press, 1978, 88.
12. See de Lubac, *Sur les Chemins de Dieu*, 192.
13. Karl Rahner, 'Experience of Self and Experience of God', *Theological Investigations*, vol. 13, London: Darton, Longman and Todd, 1975, 129.
14. Ibid., 123.
15. Karl Rahner, *Foundations of Christian Faith*, 69.
16. Emmanuel Levinas, *Totality and Infinity*, Pittsburg: Duquesne University Press/The Hague, Nijhoff, 1969, 41.
17. Ibid., 33.
18. Ibid., 58-9.
19. Ibid., 78.
20. Ibid., 75.
21. Martin Heidegger, *Identity and Difference*, New York: Stanbaugh, 1969, 72.
22. Richard Kearney, *Poetique du Possible,* Paris: Beauchesne, 1984, esp. chapter 12, 223-50.
23. Ibid., esp. chapter 12.
24. This distinction is made by E. Bloch (*Das Prinzip Hoffnung*) and used to good effect by Kearney, op. cit.
25. 1 Thess. 5:15.
26. J. B. Metz, 'The Future in the Memory of Suffering', *Concilium*, vol. 6, no. 8 (June 1972, *The God Question*), 16.
27. Ibid., 20.
28. E. Schillebeeckx, *Christ.*, 754.
29. Cited by Schillebeeckx, *Christ*, 752.
30. E. Schillebeeckx, *God, The Future of Man*, London-Sydney: Sheed and Ward, 1969, 185.

Chapter 8. Theism Revisited. A presence in Absence, pp. 132-51.
1. 'God, when thought to be absent, is seen; when present, God is not seen.' Augustine of Hippo, *De Videndo Deo (Epist.* 147, *ad Paulinam)*, c. VI, n. 18 (P.L., 33, 604).
2. 'God is best known in our not-knowing.' Augústine of Hippo, *De Ordine*, 11, 16 (P.L. 32, 1015).
3. John Courtney Murray, *The Problem of God*, 73.
4. Cited by John Macquarrie in *In Search of Deity*, 90.
5. *Summa Theologiae*, Ia., q.29, art. 3.
6. See Norman Pittenger, *Picturing God*, 12, citing A.N. Whitehead.

7. Karl Rahner, 'Theos in the New Testament', *Theological Investigations*, vol. 1, London: Darton, Longman and Todd, 1961, 117.
8. 1 Cor. 8:6; Acts 17:27-8; 1 Cor. 12:6; Rom. 1:20-22.
9. Karl Rahner, 'Theos in the New Testament', op. cit., 103.
10. Paul Tillich, *The Courage to Be*, London: Fontana, Collins, 1972, 179.
11. Macquarrie, *In Search of Deity*, 34.
12. Ibid., 53.
13. Pierre Teilhard de Chardin, *Hymn of the Universe*, London: Collins, 1965, 26-7.
14. J. A. T. Robinson, *Exploration into God*, London: SCM, 1967, 93-110.
15. E. Schillebeeckx, *Christ*, 811.
16. Ibid., 809.
17. Ibid., 639.
18. See the detail on the cover of G. Gutiérrez, *A Theology of Liberation*, New York: Orbis, 1973.
19. Simone Weil, *Gateway to God*, London: Fontana, Collins, 1974, passim.
20. Elie Wiesel, *A Jew Today*, New York: Random House (Vintage), 1979, 7.
21. Walter Brueggemann, *The Land*, Philadelphia: Fortress, 1977. 104.

Chapter 9. In the End, God—Father, Son and Blessed Spirit, pp. 152-74.
1. J. Moltmann, *The Trinity and the Kingdom of God*, London: SCM, 1981, 49.
2. F. Dostoyevsky, *The Brothers Karamazov*, (trans. D. Magarshack), Harmondsworth: Penguin, 1958, 27.
3. David Hume, *Dialogues Concerning Natural Religion*, ed. H.D. Aiken, New York: Harper, 1948, part 10, 66.
4. Hugo Meynell, *Grace versus Nature*, London-Melbourne: Sheed and Ward, 1965, 90.
5. Austin Farrer, *Love Almighty and Ills unlimited*, London: Fontana, Collins, 1966, 88.
6. Herbert McCabe, *God Matters*, London: Chapman, 1987, 34.
7. A. Farrer, op. cit., 99.
8. H. McCabe, op. cit., 33.
9. Cf. St Thomas Aquinas, *Summa Theol.*, Ia., q.48, art. I (c); also F. C. Copleston, *Aquinas*, Harmondsworth: Penguin, 1955, 147.
10. St Thomas Aquinas, *Contra Gentes*, III, 71.
11. Anthony Flew, *New Essays in Philosophical Theology*, London: SCM, 1966, 147.
12. Walter Kasper, *The God of Jesus Christ*, London: SCM, 1983, 197.
13. Dorothy Soelle, *Suffering*, London: Darton, Longman and Todd, 1975, 32.
14. Cf. Kasper, op. cit., 190.
15. Ignatius, *Ad Polycarpum*, 3, 2: Tertullian, *Adv Marcionem* II, 163: Origen, *Homilae in Ezechielem*, 6, 6.
16. Elie Wiesel, *Night*, (trans. Stella Rodway), London: Fontana, Collins, 1972, 76-7.
17. Elie Wiesel, *The Town Beyond the Wall*, (trans. Stephen Barker), New York: Avon, 1970, 174.

18. J. B. Metz, 'Facing the Jews: Christian Theology after Auschwitz' in *The Holocaust as Interruption*, 29-30.
19. *Summa Theol.* Ia., q.21, art. 3 (c).
20. See Jurgen Moltmann, *The Crucified God*, op. cit., 215.
21. *The Crucified God*, 274.
22. Jürgen Moltmann, *The Trinity and the Kingdom of God*, op. cit., 27.
23. *The Crucified God*, 246.
24. K. Rahner, 'Remarks on the Dogmatic Treatise "De Trinitate"' in *Theological Investigations*, IV, London: Darton, Longman and Todd, 1966, 96.
25. W. Kasper, *The God of Jesus Christ*, 195; J. Moltmann, *The Trinity and the Kingdom of God*, 32.
26. J. Moltmann, *The Crucified God*, 243.
27. Denis Edwards, *Human Experience of God*, New York: Paulist Press, 1983, 47.
28. Herbert McCabe, *God Matters*, 100.
29. G. O. Hanlon, 'Does God Change', in *Irish Theological Quarterly* 3 (1987), 163.
30. H. McCabe, op. cit., 109.

Appendix, Knowledge of God is the Practice of Justice, pp. 175-81.
1. Jer. 2:27.
2. Ps. 12:6 quoted by David Rosen in 'My God and God of my Fathers', *The Furrow* (July 1984), 428.
3. Walter Brueggemann, *The Land*, 107.
4. Luke 4: 16-21 = Is. 61:1-2.
5. Franz Mussner, *Tractate on the Jews. The Significance of Judaism for Christian Faith*, Philadelphia: Fortress Press, 1984, 89.
6. F. Mussner, op. cit., 79, citing G. Scholem, 'Towards an Understanding of the Messianic Idea in Judaism', in *The Messianic Idea in Judaism*, ed. G. Scholem, New York, 1971, 35 et seq.